The OFFICIAL HIGHWAY CODE
for Northern Ireland

© Crown copyright 2015

This publication is licensed under the terms of the Open Government Licence v3.0 except where otherwise stated.

To view this licence, visit **nationalarchives.gov.uk/doc/open-government-licence/version/3** or write to the Information Policy Team, The National Archives, Kew, London TW9 4DU, or email psi@nationalarchives.gsi.gov.uk

The publication of facsimile versions of this publication or any other versions that closely resemble the style and appearance of the original may confuse the public. Any publisher wishing to reproduce the content of this publication should not replicate the official version's style and appearance. Other versions should not be presented as being an official version.

Where we have identified any third-party copyright information you will need to obtain permission from the copyright holders concerned.

Material used from this document/publication must be acknowledged as Crown copyright and you must give the title of the source document/publication.

Prepared by the Department for Infrastructure.

This document/publication is also available at www.nidirect.gov.uk/the-highway-code

Twenty-first impression with updated cover 2023

ISBN 978 0 117 09440 6

The Department for Infrastructure recognises and values its customers. We will treat all our customers with respect and deliver our services in an objective, polite and fair way.

We're turning over a new leaf.

WORLD LAND TRUST™
www.carbonbalancedprint.com
CBP2223

MIX
Paper | Supporting responsible forestry
FSC® C002151

Contents

Introduction	3
Rules for pedestrians	5
Rules for powered wheelchairs and powered scooters	15
Rules about animals	18
Rules for cyclists	21
Rules for motorcyclists	26
Rules for drivers and motorcyclists	28
General rules, techniques and advice for all drivers and riders	34
Using the road	53
Road users requiring extra care	70
Driving in adverse weather conditions	76
Waiting and parking	80
Motorways	85
Breakdowns and incidents	91
Road works	96
Level crossings	97
Tramways	100
Light signals controlling traffic	102
Signals to other road users	103
Signals by authorised persons	104
Traffic signs	106
Road markings	114
Vehicle markings	117

Annexes

1.	You and your bicycle	118
2.	Motorcycle licence requirements	118
3.	Motor vehicle documentation, learner and restricted driver requirements	120
4.	The road user and the law	123
5.	Penalties	125
6.	Vehicle maintenance, safety and security	128
7.	First aid on the road	131
8.	Safety code for new drivers	133

Other information	135
Appendix	136
Index	141

Introduction

The Highway Code for Northern Ireland (hereafter referred to as *The Highway Code* or *the Code*) is essential reading for everyone.

The most vulnerable road users are pedestrians, particularly children, older or disabled people, cyclists, motorcyclists and horse riders. It is important that all road users are aware of *the Code* and are considerate towards each other. This applies to pedestrians as much as to drivers and riders.

Many of the rules in *the Code* are legal requirements, and if you disobey these rules you are committing a criminal offence. You may be fined, given penalty points on your licence or be disqualified from driving. In the most serious cases you may be sent to prison. Such rules are identified by the use of the words '**MUST/MUST NOT.**' In addition, each rule includes an abbreviated reference to the legislation which creates the offence. An explanation of the abbreviations is on page 124.

Although failure to comply with the other rules of *the Code* will not, in itself, cause a person to be prosecuted, *The Highway Code* may be used in evidence in any court proceedings under the Traffic Legislation (see page 124) to establish liability. This includes rules that use advisory wording such as 'should/should not' or 'do/do not'.

Knowing and applying the rules contained in *The Highway Code* could significantly reduce road casualties. Cutting the number of deaths and injuries that occur on our roads every day is a responsibility we all share. *The Highway Code* can help us discharge that responsibility. Further information on driving/riding techniques can be found in *The Official DVSA Guide to Driving – the essential skills*, and *The Official DVSA Guide to Riding – the essential skills*.

The Highway Code is based on the Great Britain version. Although Northern Ireland road safety legislation continues to be brought into line with that in Great Britain, there are some differences which it has been necessary to reflect in this issue. For example, many Northern Ireland road users may not be familiar with equestrian crossings or trams. References to these issues have however been included as Northern Ireland residents who plan to visit Great Britain might find them helpful. It is recommended that anyone, especially drivers, intending to visit Great Britain should also purchase the Great Britain version of *The Highway Code*. It is also recommended that anyone intending to visit the Republic of Ireland should purchase a copy of 'Rules of the Road' and note particularly that all speed limit signs in the Republic of Ireland relate to kilometres per hour. The Great Britain Highway Code is available online at www.gov.uk under Driving and transport. The Republic of Ireland Rules of the Road is available at www.rsa.ie/services/learner-drivers/resources/rules-of-the-road

Rules for pedestrians

General guidance

1 **Footways or footpaths** (including any path along the side of a road) should be used if provided. Where possible, avoid being next to the kerb with your back to the traffic. If you have to step into the road, look both ways first. Always show due care and consideration for others.

2 **If there is no footway or footpath,** walk on the right-hand side of the road so you can see oncoming traffic. You should take extra care and

- be prepared to walk in single file, especially on narrow roads or in poor light
- keep close to the side of the road.

It may be safer to cross the road well before a sharp right-hand bend so that oncoming traffic has a better chance of seeing you. Cross back after the bend.

3 **Help other road users to see you.** Wear or carry something light-coloured, bright or fluorescent in poor daylight conditions. When it is dark, use reflective materials (e.g. armbands, sashes, waistcoats, jackets, footwear), which can be seen by drivers using headlights up to three times as far away as non-reflective materials.

Rule 3
Help yourself to be seen

4 **Young children** should not be out alone on the footway, footpath or road (see Rule 7). When taking children out, keep between them and the traffic and hold their hands firmly. Strap very young children into push-chairs or use reins. When pushing a young child in a buggy, do not push the buggy into the road when checking to see if it is clear to cross, particularly from between parked vehicles.

5 **Organised walks.** Large groups of people walking together should use a footway or footpath if available; if one is not, they should keep to the left. Look-outs should be positioned at the front and back of the group and they should wear fluorescent clothes in daylight and reflective clothes in the dark. At night the look-out in front should show a white light and the one at the back a red light. People on the outside of large groups should also carry lights and wear reflective clothing.

6 **Motorways.** Pedestrians **MUST NOT** be on motorways or slip roads except in an emergency (see Rules 271 and 275).

Laws RO Art 20 & MTR reg 13(1)(b)

Crossing the road

7 **The Green Cross Code.** The advice given below for crossing the road is for all pedestrians. Children should be taught the Code and should not be allowed out alone until they can understand and use it properly. The age when they can do this is different for each child. Many children cannot judge how fast vehicles are going or how far away they are. Children learn by example, so parents and carers should always use the Code in full when out with their children. They are responsible for deciding at what age children can use it safely by themselves.

A. First find a safe place to cross and where there is a space to reach the footway or footpath on the other side. Where there is a crossing nearby, use it. It is safer to cross using a subway, a footbridge, an island, a zebra, pelican, toucan or puffin crossing, or where there is a crossing point controlled by a police officer or school

Rules for pedestrians

crossing patrol. Otherwise choose a place where you can see clearly in all directions. Try to avoid crossing between parked cars (see Rule 14), on a blind bend or close to the brow of a hill. Move to a space where drivers and riders can see you clearly. Do not cross the road diagonally.

B. Stop just before you get to the kerb, where you can see if anything is coming. Do not get too close to the traffic. If there's no footway or footpath keep back from the edge of the road but make sure you can still see approaching traffic.

Rule 7
Look all around and listen for traffic before crossing

C. Look all around for traffic and listen. Traffic could come from any direction. Listen as well, because you can sometimes hear traffic before you see it.

D. If traffic is coming, let it pass. Look all around again and listen. Do not cross until there is a safe gap in the traffic and you are certain that there is plenty of time. Remember, even if traffic is a long way off, it may be approaching very quickly.

E. When it is safe go straight across the road – do not run. Keep looking and listening for traffic while you cross, in case there is any traffic you did not see, or in case other traffic appears suddenly. Look out for cyclists and motorcyclists travelling between lanes of traffic. Do not walk diagonally across the road.

8 **At a junction.** When crossing the road, look out for traffic turning into the road, especially from behind you. If you have started and traffic wants to turn into the road, you have priority and they should give way (see Rule 170).

9 **Pedestrian safety barriers.** Where there are barriers, cross the road only at the gaps provided for pedestrians. Do not climb over the barriers or walk between them and the road.

10 **Tactile paving.** Raised surfaces that can be felt underfoot provide warning and guidance to blind or partially sighted people. The most common surfaces are a series of raised studs, which are used at crossing points with a dropped kerb, or a series of rounded raised bars which are used at level crossings, at the top and bottom of steps and at some other hazards.

11 **One-way streets.** Check which way the traffic is moving. Do not cross until it is safe to do so without stopping. Bus and cycle lanes may operate in the opposite direction to the rest of the traffic.

12 **Bus and cycle lanes.** Take care when crossing these lanes as traffic may be moving faster than in other lanes, or against the flow of traffic.

13 **Routes shared with cyclists.** Some cycle tracks run alongside footways or footpaths, using a segregating feature to separate cyclists from people on foot. Segregated routes may also incorporate short lengths of tactile paving to help visually impaired people stay on the correct side. On the pedestrian side this will comprise a series of flat-topped bars running across the direction of travel (ladder pattern). On the cyclist side the same bars are orientated in the direction of travel (tramline pattern). Not all routes which are shared with cyclists are segregated. Take extra care where this is so (see Rule 62).

Rules for pedestrians

14 **Parked vehicles.** If you have to cross between parked vehicles, use the outside edges of the vehicles as if they were the kerb. Stop there and make sure you can see all around and make sure the traffic can see you. Make sure there is a gap between any parked vehicles on the other side so you can reach the footway or footpath. Never cross the road in front of, or behind, any vehicle with its engine running, especially a large vehicle, as the driver may not be able to see you.

15 **Reversing vehicles.** Never cross behind a vehicle that is reversing, showing white reversing lights or sounding a warning.

16 **Moving vehicles.** You **MUST NOT** get on to or hold on to a moving vehicle.
Law RTO 1995 Art 37

17 **At night**. Wear something reflective to make it easier for others to see you (see Rule 3). If there is no pedestrian crossing nearby, cross the road near a street light so that traffic can see you more easily.

Crossings

18 **At all crossings.** When using any type of crossing you should

- always check that the traffic has stopped before you start to cross or push a pram onto the crossing
- always cross between the studs or over the zebra markings. Do not cross at the side of the crossing or on the zigzag lines, as it can be dangerous.

You **MUST NOT** loiter on any type of crossing.

Laws RTRO Art 59(4) & PCR reg 17

19 **Zebra crossings.** Give traffic plenty of time to see you and to stop before you cross. Vehicles will need more time when the road is slippery. Wait until traffic has stopped from both directions or the road is clear before crossing. Remember that traffic does not have to stop until someone has moved onto the crossing. Keep looking both ways, and listening, in case a driver or rider has not seen you and attempts to overtake a vehicle that has stopped.

Rule 19 Zebra crossings have flashing beacons

20 Where there is an island in the middle of a zebra crossing, wait on the island and follow Rule 19 before you cross the second half of the road – it is a separate crossing.

Rule 20 Zebra crossings with a central island are two separate crossings

21 **At traffic lights.** There may be special signals for pedestrians. You should only start to cross the road when the green figure shows. If you have started to cross the road and the green figure goes out, you should still

Rules for pedestrians

have time to reach the other side, but do not delay. If no pedestrian signals have been provided, watch carefully and do not cross until the traffic lights are red and the traffic has stopped. Keep looking and check for traffic that may be turning the corner. Remember that traffic lights may let traffic move in some lanes while traffic in other lanes has stopped.

Rule 21
At traffic lights, puffin and pelican crossings

*At pelican crossings only

Do not cross | Cross with care | Do not start to cross*

22 **Pelican crossings.** These are signal-controlled crossings operated by pedestrians. Push the control button to activate the traffic signals. When the red figure shows, do not cross. When a steady green figure shows, check that traffic has stopped then cross with care. When the green figure begins to flash you should not cross. If you have already started you should have time to finish crossing safely.

23 **Puffin crossings** differ from pelican crossings as the red and green figures are above the control box on your side of the road and there is no flashing green figure phase. Press the button and wait for the green figure to show.

24 When the road is congested, traffic on your side of the road may be forced to stop even though their lights are green. Traffic may still be moving on the other side of the road, so press the button and wait for the signal to cross.

25 **Toucan crossings** are light-controlled crossings which allow cyclists and pedestrians to share crossing space and cross at the same time. They are push-button operated. Cyclists are permitted to ride across.

Rule 25
Toucan crossings can be used by both cyclists and pedestrians

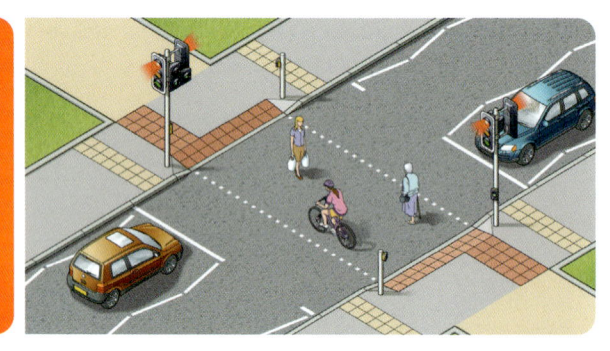

26 At some crossings there is a bleeping sound or voice signal to indicate to blind or partially sighted people when the steady green figure is showing, and there may be a tactile signal to help deafblind people.

27 **Equestrian crossings** are for horse riders. They have pavement barriers, wider crossing spaces, horse and rider figures in the light panels and either two sets of controls (one higher), or just one higher control panel.

Rule 27
Equestrian crossings are used by horse riders. There is often a parallel crossing

Rules for pedestrians

28 **'Staggered' pelican or puffin crossings.** When the crossings on each side of the central refuge are not in line they are two separate crossings. On reaching the central island press the button again and wait for a steady green figure.

Rule 28 Staggered crossings (with an island in the middle) are two separate crossings

29 **Crossings controlled by an authorised person.** Do not cross the road unless you are signalled to do so by a police officer or school crossing patrol. Always cross in front of them.

30 Where there are no controlled crossing points available it is advisable to cross where there is an island in the middle of the road. Use the Green Cross Code (see Rule 7) to cross to the island then stop and use it again to cross the second half of the road.

Situations needing extra care

31 **Emergency vehicles.** If an ambulance, fire engine, police or any other emergency vehicle approaches using flashing blue lights, headlights and/or sirens, keep off the road.

32 **Buses.** Get on or off a bus only when it has stopped to allow you to do so. Watch out for cyclists when you are getting off. Never cross the road directly behind or in front of a bus. Wait until it has moved off and you can see the road clearly in both directions.

33 **Tramways.** These may run through pedestrian areas. Their path will be marked out by shallow kerbs, changes in the paving or other road surface, white lines or yellow dots. Cross at designated crossings where provided. Elsewhere treat trams as you would other vehicles and look both ways along the track before crossing. Do not walk along the track as trams may come up behind you. Trams move quietly and cannot steer to avoid you.

34 **Railway level crossings.** You **MUST NOT** cross or pass a stop line when the red lights show, (including a red pedestrian figure). Also do not cross if an alarm is sounding or the barriers are being lowered. The tone of the alarm may change if another train is approaching. If there are no lights, alarms or barriers, stop, look both ways and listen before crossing. A tactile surface comprising rounded bars running across the direction of pedestrian travel may be installed on the footway or footpath approaching a level crossing to warn visually impaired people of its presence. The tactile surface should extend across the full width of the footway or footpath and should be located at an appropriate distance from the barrier or projected line of the barrier.

Law TSR reg 39

35 **Street, footway and footpath repairs.** A footway or footpath may be closed temporarily because it is not safe to use. Take extra care if you are directed to walk on or to cross the road.

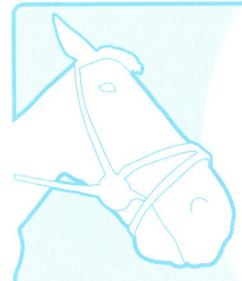

Where should horse riders be when using roundabouts?

Turn to rule 187 (page 65)

Rules for users of powered wheelchairs and powered mobility scooters

(Called Invalid Carriages in law)

36 There is one class of manual wheelchair (called a Class 1 Invalid Carriage) and two classes of powered wheelchairs and powered mobility scooters. Manual wheelchairs and Class 2 vehicles are those with an upper speed limit of 4 mph (6 km/h) and are designed to be used on footways or footpaths. Class 3 vehicles are those with an upper speed limit of 8mph (12 km/h) and are equipped to be used on the road as well as footways or footpaths.

37 When you are on the road you should obey the guidance and rules for other vehicles; when on the footway or footpath you should follow the guidance and rules for pedestrians.

On footways or footpaths

38 Footways or footpaths are safer than roads and should be used when available. You should give pedestrians priority and show consideration for other footway or footpath users, particularly those with a hearing or visual impairment who may not be aware that you are there.

39 Powered wheelchairs and scooters **MUST NOT** travel faster than 4 mph (6 km/h) on footways or footpaths or in pedestrian areas. You may need to reduce your speed to adjust to other footway or footpath users who may not be able to move out of your way quickly enough or where the footway or footpath is too narrow.

Law MV(IC)R reg 4

40 When moving off the footway or footpath onto the road you should take special care. Before moving off, always look round and make sure it's safe to join the traffic. Always try to use dropped kerbs when moving off the footway or footpath, even if this means travelling further to locate one. If you have to climb or descend a kerb, always approach it at right angles and don't try to negotiate a kerb higher than the vehicle manufacturer's recommendations.

On the road

41 You should take care when travelling on the road as you may be travelling more slowly than other traffic (your machine is restricted to 8 mph (12 km/h) and may be less visible).

42 When on the road, Class 3 vehicles should travel in the direction of the traffic. Class 2 users should always use the footway or footpath when it is available. When there is no footway or footpath, you should use caution when on the road. Class 2 users should, where possible, travel in the direction of the traffic as this is safer. If you are travelling at night, when lights **MUST** be used, you should travel in the direction of the traffic to avoid confusing other road users.

Law MV(IC)R reg 9

43 You **MUST** follow the same rules about using lights, indicators and horns as for other road vehicles if your vehicle is fitted with them. At night lights **MUST** be used. Be aware that other road users may not be able to see you and you should make yourself more visible – even in the daytime and also at dusk – by, for instance, wearing a reflective jacket or reflective strips on the back of the vehicle.

Law MV(IC)R reg 9

What should you do if the traffic lights are not working?

Turn to rule 176 (page 61)

Rules for users of powered wheelchairs and powered mobility scooters

44 Take extra care at road junctions. When going straight ahead, check to make sure there are no vehicles about to cross your path from the left, the right, or overtaking you and turning left. There are several options for dealing with right turns, especially turning from a major road. If moving into the middle of the road is difficult or dangerous, you can

- stop on the left hand side of the road and wait for a safe gap in the traffic
- negotiate the turn as a pedestrian, i.e. travel along the footway or footpath and cross the road between the footways or footpaths where it is safe to do so. Class 3 users should switch the vehicle to the lower speed limit when on footways or footpaths.

If the junction is too hazardous, it may be worth considering an alternative route. Similarly, when negotiating major roundabouts (i.e. with two or more lanes) it may be safer for you to use the footway or footpath or find a route which avoids the roundabout altogether.

45 All normal parking restrictions should be observed. Your vehicle should not be left unattended if it causes an obstruction to other pedestrians – especially those in wheelchairs. Parking concessions provided under the Blue Badge scheme (see page 136) will apply to those vehicles displaying a valid badge.

46 These vehicles **MUST NOT** be used on motorways (see Rule 253). They should not be used on unrestricted dual carriageways where the speed limit exceeds 50 mph (80 km/h) but if they are used on these dual carriageways, they **MUST** have a flashing amber beacon. A flashing amber beacon should be used on other dual carriageways (see Rule 220).

Laws RO Art 20(1), (3) & (4), & RVLR regs 20(1) & 29

Rules about animals

Horse-drawn vehicles

47 Horse-drawn vehicles used on the road should be operated and maintained in accordance with standards set out in the Department for Transport's Code of Practice for Horse-Drawn Vehicles. This Code lays down the requirements for a road driving assessment in Great Britain and includes a comprehensive list of safety checks to ensure that a carriage and its fittings are safe and in good working order.

48 **Safety equipment and clothing.** All horse drawn vehicles should have two red rear reflectors. It is safer not to drive at night but if you do, a light showing white to the front and red to the rear **MUST** be fitted.

Law RVLR reg 4

Horse riders

49 **Safety equipment.** Children under the age of 14 **MUST** wear a helmet which complies with the Regulations. It **MUST** be fastened securely. Other riders should also follow these requirements. These requirements do not apply to a child who is a follower of the Sikh religion while wearing a turban.

Laws H(PHYR)O Art 3 & H(PHYR)R

50 **Other clothing.** You should wear

- boots or shoes with hard soles and heels
- light-coloured or fluorescent clothing in daylight
- reflective clothing if you have to ride at night or in poor visibility.

Rule 50
Help yourself to be seen

51 **At night.** It is safer not to ride on the road at night or in poor visibility, but if you do, make sure your horse has reflective bands above the fetlock joints. A light which shows white to the front and red to the rear should be fitted, with a band, to the rider's right arm and/or leg/riding boot. If you are leading a horse at night, carry a light in your right hand showing white to the front and red to the rear and wear reflective clothing on both you and your horse. It is strongly recommended that a fluorescent/reflective tail guard is also worn by your horse.

Riding

52 Before you take a horse on to a road you should

- ensure all tack fits well and is in good condition
- make sure you can control the horse.

Always ride with other, less nervous horses if you think that your horse will be nervous of traffic. Never ride a horse without both a saddle and bridle.

53 Before riding off or turning, always look behind you to make sure it is safe, then give a clear arm signal.

When riding on the road you should

- keep to the left
- keep both hands on the reins unless you are signalling
- keep both feet in the stirrups

- not carry another person
- not carry anything which might affect your balance or get tangled up with the reins
- keep a horse you are leading to the left
- move in the direction of the traffic flow in a one-way street
- never ride more than two abreast, and ride in single file on narrow or busy roads and when riding around bends.

54 You should not take a horse on to a footway, footpath or cycle track. In Great Britain, use a bridleway where possible. In Great Britain equestrian crossings may be provided for horse riders to cross the road and you should use these where available (see Rule 27). You should dismount at level crossings where a 'Horse Rider Dismount' sign is displayed.

55 Avoid roundabouts wherever possible. If you use them you should

- keep to your left and watch out for vehicles crossing your path to leave or join the roundabout
- signal right when riding across exits to show you are not leaving
- signal left just before you leave the roundabout.

Other animals

56 **Dogs.** Do not let a dog out on the road on its own. Keep it on a short lead when walking on the footway, footpath, road or path shared with cyclists or horse riders.

57 When in a vehicle, make sure that dogs and other animals are suitably restrained so they cannot distract you while you are driving or injure you, or themselves if you stop quickly. A seat belt harness, pet carrier, dog cage or dog guard are ways of restraining animals in cars.

58 **Animals being herded.** These should be kept under control at all times. You should, if possible, send another person along the road in front to warn other road users, especially at a bend or the brow of a hill. It is safer not to move animals after dark, but if you do, then wear reflective clothing and ensure that lights are carried (white at the front and red at the rear of the herd).

Rules for cyclists

These rules are in addition to those in the following sections, which apply to all vehicles (except the motorway section on page 85). See also on page 118 – You and your bicycle.

59 **Clothing.** You should wear in the correct size and securely fastened

- a cycle helmet which conforms to current regulations
- appropriate clothes for cycling. Avoid clothes that may get tangled in the chain, or in a wheel or may obscure your lights
- light-coloured or fluorescent clothing which helps other road users see you in daylight and poor light
- reflective clothing and/or accessories (belt, arm or ankle bands) in the dark.

Rule 59 Help yourself to be seen

60 **Between sunset and sunrise** your cycle **MUST** have white front and red rear lights lit. It **MUST** also be fitted with a red rear reflector (and amber pedal reflectors, if manufactured after 24/1/96). White front reflectors and spoke reflectors will also help you to be seen. Flashing lights are permitted but it is recommended that cyclists who are riding in areas without street lighting use a steady front lamp.

Law RVLR regs 13, 15, 21 & 27 (as amended by RVL(A)R)

When cycling

61 **Cycle routes and other facilities.** Use cycle routes, advanced stop lines, cycle boxes and toucan crossings unless at the time it is unsafe to do so. Use of these facilities is not compulsory and will depend on your experience and skills, but they can make your journey safer.

62 **Cycle tracks.** These are normally located away from the road but may also be found alongside footways or footpaths. Cyclists or pedestrians may be segregated or they may share the same space (unsegregated). When using segregated tracks you **MUST** keep to the side intended for cyclists as the pedestrian side remains a footway or footpath. Take care when passing pedestrians, especially children, older or disabled people, and allow them plenty of room. Always be prepared to slow down and stop if necessary. Take care near road junctions as you may have difficulty seeing other road users, who might not notice you.

Law RTRO Arts 3 & 4(5)

63 **Cycle lanes.** These are marked by a white line (which may be broken) along the carriageway (see Rule 140). When using a cycle lane, keep within the lane when practicable. Before leaving a cycle lane check that it is safe to do so and signal your intention clearly to other road users. Use of cycle lanes is not compulsory and will depend on your experience and skills, but they can make your journey safer.

Rules for cyclists

64 You **MUST NOT** cycle on a footway or footpath unless on a cycle track where one has been provided.
Law RTRO Art 3

65 **Bus lanes.** Most bus lanes, excluding motorway bus lanes, may be used by motorcyclists and cyclists as indicated on signs. Watch out for people getting on or off a bus. Be very careful when overtaking a bus or leaving a bus lane as you will be entering a busier traffic flow.

66 You should

- keep both hands on the handlebars except when signalling or changing gear
- keep both feet on the pedals
- never ride more than two abreast, and ride in single file on narrow or busy roads or when riding round bends
- not ride close behind another vehicle
- not carry anything that will affect your balance or may get caught up with your wheels or chain
- be considerate of other road users, particularly blind and partially sighted pedestrians. Let them know you are there when necessary, for example by sounding your bell or horn.

67 You should

- look all around before moving away from the kerb, turning or manoeuvring, to make sure it is safe to do so. Give a clear signal to show other road users what you intend to do (see page 103)
- look well ahead for obstructions in the road, such as drains, pot-holes and parked vehicles so that you do not have to swerve suddenly to avoid them. Leave plenty of room when passing parked vehicles and watch out for doors being opened or pedestrians stepping into your path
- be aware of traffic coming up behind you
- take extra care near road humps, narrowings and other traffic calming features
- take care when overtaking (see Rules 162–169).

68 You **MUST NOT**

- carry a passenger unless your cycle has been built or adapted to carry one
- hold on to a moving vehicle or trailer
- ride in a dangerous, careless or inconsiderate manner
- ride when under the influence of drink or drugs including medicine.

Law RTO 1995 Arts 35, 37, 42, 43 & 44

69 You **MUST** obey all traffic signs and traffic light signals.

Laws RTO 1995 Art 50 & TSR reg 8

70 When parking your cycle

- find a conspicuous location where it can be seen by passers-by
- use cycle stands or other cycle parking facilities wherever possible
- do not leave it where it would cause an obstruction or hazard to other road users
- secure it well so that it will not fall over and become an obstruction or hazard.

71 You **MUST NOT** cross the stop line when the traffic lights are red. Some junctions have an advanced stop line to enable you to wait and position yourself ahead of other traffic (see Rule 178).

Laws RTO 1995 Art 50 & TSR reg 33(1)

Road junctions

72 **On the left.** When approaching a junction on the left, watch out for vehicles turning in front of you, out of or into the side road. Just before you turn, check for undertaking cyclists or motorcyclists. Do not ride on the inside of vehicles signalling or slowing down to turn left.

Rules for cyclists

73 Pay particular attention to long vehicles, which need a lot of room to manoeuvre at corners. Be aware that drivers may not see you. They may have to move over to the right before turning left. Wait until they have completed the manoeuvre because the rear wheels come very close to the kerb while turning. Do not be tempted to ride in the space between them and the kerb.

74 **On the right**. If you are turning right, check the traffic to ensure it is safe, then signal and move to the centre of the road. Wait until there is a safe gap in the oncoming traffic before completing the turn. It may be safer to wait on the left until there is a safe gap or to dismount and push your cycle across the road.

75 **Dual carriageways**. Remember that traffic on most dual carriageways moves quickly. When crossing, wait for a safe gap and cross each carriageway in turn. Take extra care when crossing slip roads.

Roundabouts

76 Full details about the correct procedure at roundabouts are contained in rules 184–190 and in the Appendix on pages 136–140. Roundabouts can be hazardous and should be approached with care.

77 You may feel safer walking your cycle round on the footway, footpath or verge. If you decide to keep to the left you should

- be aware that drivers may not easily see you
- take extra care when cycling across exits. You may need to signal right to show you are not leaving the roundabout
- watch out for vehicles crossing your path to leave or join the roundabout.

78 Give plenty of room to long vehicles on the roundabout as they need more room to manoeuvre. Do not ride in the space they need to get round the roundabout. It may be safer to wait until they have cleared the roundabout.

Crossing the road

79 Do not ride across equestrian crossings, as they are for horse riders only. Do not ride across a pelican, puffin or zebra crossing. Dismount and wheel your cycle across.

80 **Toucan crossings**. These are light-controlled crossings, which allow cyclists and pedestrians to share crossing space and cross at the same time. They are push-button operated. Pedestrians and cyclists will see the green signal together. Cyclists are permitted to ride across.

81 **Cycle-only crossings**. Cycle tracks on opposite sides of the road may be linked by signalled crossings. You may ride across but you **MUST NOT** cross until the green cycle symbol is showing.

Law TSR reg 33(1)

82 **Level crossings/Tramways**. Take extra care when crossing the tracks (see Rule 306). You should dismount at level crossings where a 'Cyclist Dismount' sign is displayed.

Rules for motorcyclists

These rules are in addition to those in the following sections, which apply to all vehicles. For motorcycle licence requirements see pages 118–119.

83 On all journeys, the rider and pillion passenger on a motorcycle, scooter, moped or motor quadricycle, also called quadbike, **MUST** wear a protective helmet. This does not apply to a follower of the Sikh religion while wearing a turban. Helmets **MUST** comply with the

Rules for motorcyclists

regulations and they **MUST** be fastened securely. Riders and passengers of motor tricycles should also wear a protective helmet. Before each journey check that your helmet visor is clean and in good condition.

Laws MC(PH)R (as amended) reg 2 & RTO 1995 Arts 27 & 28

84 It is also advisable to wear eye protectors, which **MUST** comply with the Regulations. Scratched or poorly fitting eye protectors can limit your view when riding, particularly in bright sunshine and the hours of darkness. Consider wearing ear protectors. Strong boots, gloves and suitable clothing may help to protect you if you are involved in a collision.

Laws MC(EP)R (as amended) reg 2 & RTO 1995 Art 29

85 You **MUST NOT** carry more than one pillion passenger, who **MUST** sit astride the machine on a proper seat. They should face forward with both feet on the footrests. You **MUST NOT** carry a pillion passenger unless your motorcycle is designed to do so. Provisional licence holders **MUST NOT** carry a pillion passenger.

Laws RTO 1995 Art 34, MV(DL)R reg 12(5) & CUR reg 118

86 **Daylight riding**. Make yourself as visible as possible from the side as well as the front and the rear. You could wear a light or brightly coloured helmet and fluorescent clothing or strips. Dipped headlights, even in good daylight, may also make you more conspicuous. However, be aware that other vehicle drivers may still not have seen you, or judged your distance or speed correctly, especially at junctions.

Rule 86 Help yourself to be seen

87 **Riding in the dark**. Wear reflective clothing or strips to improve your visibility in the dark. These reflect the light from the headlamps of other vehicles, making you visible from a long distance. See Rules 113–116 for lighting requirements.

88 **Manoeuvring**. You should be aware of what is behind and to the sides before manoeuvring. Look behind you; use mirrors if they are fitted. When in traffic queues, look out for pedestrians crossing between vehicles and vehicles emerging from junctions, or changing lanes. Position yourself so that drivers can see you in their mirrors. Additionally, when filtering in slow-moving traffic, take care and keep your speed low.

Remember: Observation–Signal–Manoeuvre

Rules for drivers and motorcyclists

89 **Vehicle condition**. You **MUST** ensure your vehicle and trailer comply with the full requirements of the Motor Vehicles (Construction and Use) Regulations (NI) and the Road Vehicles Lighting Regulations (NI) (see page 124).

Laws CUR, RVLR

Fitness to drive

90 Make sure that you are fit to drive. You **MUST** report to the Driver and Vehicle Agency any health condition likely to affect your driving.

Law RTO 1981 Art 11

91 Driving when you are tired greatly increases your risk of collision. To minimise this risk
- make sure you are fit to drive. Do not begin a journey if you are tired. Get a good night's sleep before embarking on a long journey
- avoid undertaking long journeys between midnight and 6am, when natural alertness is at a minimum

Rules for drivers and motorcyclists

- plan your journey to take sufficient breaks. A minimum break of at least 15 minutes after every two hours of driving is recommended
- if you feel at all sleepy, stop in a safe place. Do not stop on the hard shoulder of a motorway
- the most effective ways to counter sleepiness are to drink, for example, two cups of caffeinated coffee and to take a short nap (up to 15 minutes).

92 **Vision**. You **MUST** be able to read a vehicle number plate, in good daylight, from a distance of 20 metres (or 20.5 metres where the old style number plate is used). If you need to wear glasses (or contact lenses) to do this, you **MUST** wear them at all times while driving. The police have the power to require a driver to undertake an eyesight test.

Laws RTO 1981 Art 154, MV(DL)R reg 29 & sch 7, & MVDL(A)R

93 Slow down, and if necessary stop, if you are dazzled by bright sunlight.

94 At night or in poor visibility, do not use tinted glasses, lenses or visors if they restrict your vision.

Alcohol and drugs

95 **Do not drink and drive** as it will seriously affect your judgement and abilities. You **MUST NOT** drive with a breath alcohol level higher than 35 microgrammes/100 millilitres of breath or a blood alcohol level of more than 80 milligrammes/100 millilitres of blood. Alcohol will

- give a false sense of confidence
- reduce co-ordination and slow down reactions
- affect judgement of speed, distance and risk
- reduce your driving ability, even if you're below the legal limit
- take time to leave your body; you may be unfit to drive in the evening after drinking at lunchtime, or in the morning after drinking the previous evening.

The best solution is not to drink at all when driving, because any amount of alcohol can impair driving ability. If you are going to drink, arrange other means of transport.

Law RTO 1995 Arts 13, 15 & 16

96 You **MUST NOT** drive under the influence of drugs or medicine. Check the instructions or ask your doctor or pharmacist. Using illegal drugs is highly dangerous. Never take them if you intend to drive; the effects are unpredictable but can be even more severe than alcohol and may result in fatal or serious road crashes.

Law RTO 1995 Art 15

97 **Before setting off**. You should ensure that

- you have planned your route and allowed sufficient time
- clothing and footwear do not prevent you using the controls in the correct manner
- you know where all the controls are and how to use them before you need them. Not all vehicles are the same; do not wait until it is too late to find out
- your mirrors and seat are adjusted correctly to ensure comfort, full control and maximum vision
- head restraints are properly adjusted to reduce the risk of neck and spine injuries in the event of a collision
- you have sufficient fuel before commencing your journey, especially if it includes motorway driving. It can be dangerous to lose power when driving in traffic
- your vehicle is legal and roadworthy
- you have switched off your mobile phone.

Rule 97 Make sure head restraints are properly adjusted

Rules for drivers and motorcyclists

98 **Vehicle towing and loading**. As a driver

- you **MUST NOT** tow more than your licence permits. If you passed a car test after 1 January 1997 you are restricted on the weight of trailer you can tow

- you **MUST NOT** overload your vehicle or trailer. You should not tow a weight greater than that recommended by the manufacturer of your vehicle

- you **MUST** secure your load and it **MUST NOT** stick out dangerously. Make sure any heavy or sharp objects and any animals are secured safely. If there is a collision, they might hit someone inside the vehicle and cause serious injury

- you should properly distribute the weight in your caravan or trailer, with heavy items mainly over the axle(s) and ensure a downward load on the tow ball. Manufacturers' recommended weight and tow ball load should not be exceeded. This should avoid the possibility of swerving or snaking and going out of control. If this does happen, ease off the accelerator and reduce speed gently to regain control

- carrying a load or pulling a trailer may require you to adjust the headlights.

In the event of a breakdown, be aware that towing a vehicle on a tow rope is potentially dangerous. You should consider professional recovery.

Laws CUR reg 115 & MV(DL)R reg 32

Seat belts and child restraints

99 **You MUST wear a seat belt** in cars, vans and other goods vehicles if one is fitted (see table below). Adults and children aged 14 years and over **MUST** use a seatbelt where fitted, when seated in minibuses, buses and coaches. Exemptions are allowed for the holders of medical exemption certificates and those making deliveries and collections in goods vehicles when travelling less than 50 metres (approx. 162 feet).

Laws RTO 1995 Arts 23 & 24, RTO 2007 Art 26, MV(WSB)R, MV(WSBCFS)R & MV(WSB)(A)R

Seat belt requirements. This table summarises the main legal requirements for wearing seatbelts in cars, vans and other goods vehicles.

	Front seat	Rear seat	Who is responsible?
Driver	Seat belt **MUST** be worn if fitted		Driver
Child under 3 years of age	Correct child restraint **MUST** be used	Correct child restraint **MUST** be used. If one is not available in a taxi the child may travel unrestrained	Driver
Child from 3rd birthday up to 1.35 metres (approx 4ft 5 inches) in height (or 12th birthday, whichever they reach first)	Correct child restraint **MUST** be used	Correct child restraint **MUST** be used where seat belts fitted. **MUST** use adult belt if correct child restraint is not available in a licensed taxi or private hire vehicle, or for reasons of unexpected necessity over a short distance, or if two occupied restraints prevent fitment of a third	Driver
Child over 1.35 metres in height or 12 or 13 years	Seat belt **MUST** be worn if available	Seat belt **MUST** be worn if available	Driver
Adult passengers aged 14 and over	Seat belt **MUST** be worn if available	Seat belt **MUST** be worn if available	Passenger

100 The driver **MUST** ensure that all children under 14 years of age in cars, vans and other goods vehicles wear seat belts or sit in an approved child restraint where required (see table above). If a child is under 1.35 metres (approx 4 feet 5 inches) tall, a baby seat, child seat, booster seat or booster cushion suitable for the child's weight and fitted to the manufacturer's instructions **MUST** be used.

Laws RTO 1995 Arts 23 & 24, MV(WSB)R, MV(WSBCFS)R & MV(WSB)(A)R

Rules for drivers and motorcyclists

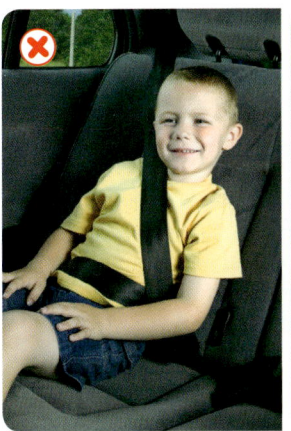

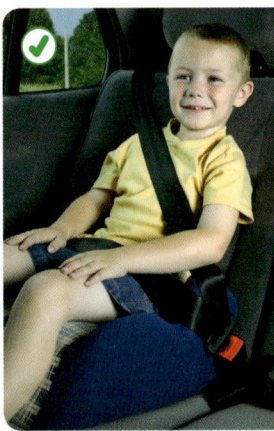

Rule 100
Make sure that a child uses a suitable restraint which is correctly adjusted

101 A rear-facing baby seat **MUST NOT** be fitted into a seat protected by an active frontal airbag, as in a crash it can cause serious injury or death to the child.

Laws RTO 1995 Arts 23 & 24, MV(WSB)R, MV(WSBCFS)R & MV(WSB)(A)R

102 **Children in cars, vans and other goods vehicles.** Drivers who are carrying children in cars, vans and other goods vehicles should also ensure that

- children should get into the vehicle through the door nearest the kerb
- child restraints are properly fitted to manufacturer's instructions
- children do not sit behind the rear seats in an estate car or hatchback, unless a special child seat has been fitted
- the child safety door locks, where fitted, are used when children are in the vehicle
- children are kept under control.

General rules, techniques and advice for all drivers and riders

This section should be read by all drivers, motorcyclists, cyclists and horse riders. The rules in *The Highway Code* do not give you the right of way in any circumstance, but they do advise you when you should give way to others. Always give way if it can help to avoid an incident.

Signals

103 Signals warn and inform other road users, including pedestrians (see page 103) of your intended actions. You should always

- give clear signals in plenty of time, having checked it is not misleading to signal at that time

- use them to advise other road users before moving off, changing course or direction or stopping

- cancel them after use

- make sure your signals will not confuse others. If, for instance, you want to stop after a side road, do not signal until you are passing the road. If you signal earlier it may give the impression that you intend to turn into the road. Your brake lights will warn traffic behind you that you are slowing down

- use an arm signal to emphasise or reinforce your signal if necessary. Remember that signalling does not give you priority.

104 You should also

- watch out for signals given by other road users and proceed only when you are satisfied that it is safe

- be aware that an indicator on another vehicle may not have been cancelled.

General rules, techniques and advice for all drivers and riders

105 You **MUST** obey signals given by police officers and Driver and Vehicle Agency Enforcement Officers (see pages 104–105) and signs used by school crossing patrols.

Laws RTRO Art 60, RTO 1995 Arts 49, 75 & 76, & RTO 1981 Arts 180 and 180A

106 **Police stopping procedures**. If police in a vehicle want to stop your vehicle, they will, where possible, attract your attention by

- flashing blue lights or headlights or sounding their siren or horn, usually from behind
- directing you to pull over to the side by pointing and/or using the left indicator.

You **MUST** then pull over and stop as soon as it is safe to do so. Then switch off your engine.

Law RTO 1981 Art 180

Other stopping procedures

107 **Driver and Vehicle Agency Enforcement Officers** have powers to stop vehicles on all roads, including motorways. They will attract your attention by flashing amber lights

- either from the front requesting you to follow them to a safe place to stop
- or from behind directing you to pull over to the side by pointing and/or using the left indicator.

It is an offence not to comply with their directions. You **MUST** obey any signals given (see page 105).

Law RTO 1981 Art 180A

108 **Traffic officers** have powers to stop vehicles on most motorways and some 'A' class roads in England and Wales. If traffic officers in uniform want to stop your vehicle on safety grounds (e.g. an insecure load) they will, where possible, attract your attention by

- flashing amber lights, usually from behind
- directing you to pull over to the side of the road by pointing and/or using the left indicator

You **MUST** then pull over and stop as soon as it is safe to do so. Then switch off your engine. It is an offence not to comply with their directions.

Law RTA 1988 sects 35 & 163 as amended by TMA sect 6

109 **Traffic light signals and traffic signs**. You **MUST** obey all traffic light signals (see page 102) and traffic signs giving orders, including temporary signals and signs (see pages 106–111). Make sure you know, understand and act on all other traffic and information signs and road markings (see pages 106–117)

Laws RTO 1995 Art 50 & TSR regs 8, 13, 14, 24, 25, 25A, 25B, 26 & 33

110 **Flashing headlights**. Only flash your headlights to let other road users know that you are there. Do not flash your headlights to convey any other message or to intimidate other road users.

111 Never assume that flashing headlights is a signal inviting you to proceed. Use your own judgement and proceed carefully.

112 **The horn**. Use only while your vehicle is moving and you need to warn other road users of your presence. Never sound your horn aggressively. You **MUST NOT** use your horn

- while stationary on the road
- when driving in a built-up area between the hours of 11.30 pm and 7.00 am

except when another road user poses a danger.

Law CUR reg 114

General rules, techniques and advice for all drivers and riders

Lighting requirements

113 You **MUST**

- ensure all sidelights and rear registration plate lights are lit between sunset and sunrise
- use headlights at night
- use headlights when visibility is seriously reduced (see Rule 226).

Night (the hours of darkness) is defined as the period between half an hour after sunset and half an hour before sunrise.

Laws RVLR regs 2, 27 & 28, & RV(DRM)R reg 9

114 You **MUST NOT**

- use any lights in a way that would dazzle or cause discomfort to other road users, including pedestrians, cyclists and horse riders
- use front or rear fog lights unless visibility is seriously reduced. You **MUST** switch them off when visibility improves to avoid dazzling other road users (see Rule 226).

In stationary queues of traffic, drivers should apply the parking brake and, once the following traffic has stopped, take their foot off the footbrake to deactivate the vehicle brake lights. This will minimise glare to road users behind until the traffic moves again.

Law RVLR reg 30

115 You should also

- use dipped headlights in dull daytime weather, to ensure that you can be seen
- keep your headlights dipped when you are overtaking until you are level with the other vehicle and then change to main beam if necessary, unless this would dazzle oncoming road users

- slow down, and if necessary stop, if dazzled by oncoming headlights.

Law RVLR reg 30

116 **Hazard warning lights**. These may be used when your vehicle is stationary, to warn that it is temporarily obstructing traffic. Never use them as an excuse for dangerous or illegal parking. You **MUST NOT** use hazard warning lights while driving or being towed unless you are on a motorway or unrestricted dual carriageway and you need to warn drivers behind you of a hazard or obstruction ahead. Only use them for long enough to ensure that your warning has been observed.

Law RVLR reg 30

Control of the vehicle

Braking

117 **In normal circumstances**. The safest way to brake is to do so early and lightly. Brake more firmly as you begin to stop. Ease the pressure off just as the vehicle comes to rest to avoid a jerky stop.

118 **In an emergency**. Brake immediately. Try to avoid braking so harshly that you lock your wheels. Locked wheels can lead to loss of control.

119 **Skids**. Skidding is usually caused by the driver braking, accelerating or steering too harshly or driving too fast for the road conditions. If skidding occurs, remove the cause by releasing the brake pedal fully or easing off the accelerator. Turn the steering wheel in the direction of the skid. For example, if the rear of the vehicle skids to the right, steer immediately to the right to recover.

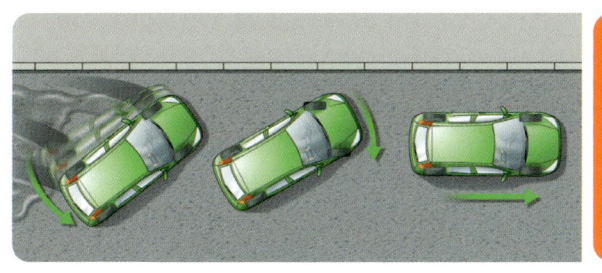

General rules, techniques and advice for all drivers and riders

Rule 119
Rear of the car skids to the right. Driver steers to the right

120 **ABS**. If your vehicle is fitted with anti-lock brakes, you should follow the advice given in the vehicle handbook. However in the case of an emergency, apply the footbrake firmly; do not release the pressure until the vehicle has slowed to the desired speed. The ABS should ensure that steering control will be retained, but do not assume that a vehicle with ABS will stop in a shorter distance.

121 **Brakes affected by water**. If you have driven through deep water your brakes may be less effective. Test them at the first safe opportunity by gently pushing on the brake pedal to make sure that they work. If they are not fully effective, gently apply light pressure while driving slowly. This will help to dry them out.

122 **Coasting**. This term describes a vehicle travelling in neutral or with the clutch pressed down. It can reduce driver control because

- engine braking is eliminated
- vehicle speed downhill will increase quickly
- increased use of the footbrake can reduce its effectiveness
- steering response will be affected, particularly on bends and corners
- it may be more difficult to select the appropriate gear when needed.

The vehicle is also less likely to be heard by other road users.

123 **The Driver and the Environment.** You **MUST NOT** leave a parked vehicle unattended with the engine running or leave a vehicle engine running unnecessarily while that vehicle is stationary on a public road. Generally, if the vehicle is stationary and likely to remain so for more than a couple of minutes you should apply the parking brake and switch off the engine to reduce emissions and noise pollution. However, it is permissible to leave the engine running if the vehicle is stationary in traffic or for diagnosing faults.

Law CUR regs 113 & 123

Speed limits

Type of vehicle	Built-up areas* mph (km/h)	Single carriageways mph (km/h)	Dual carriageways mph (km/h)	Motorways mph (km/h)
Cars & motorcycles (including car-derived vans up to 2 tonnes maximum laden weight)	30 (48)	60 (96)	70 (112)	70 (112)
Cars towing caravans or trailers (including car-derived vans and motorcycles)	30 (48)	50 (80)	60 (96)	60 (96)
Buses, coaches and minibuses (not exceeding 12 metres in overall length)	30 (48)	50 (80)	60 (96)	70 (112)
Goods vehicles (not exceeding 7.5 tonnes maximum laden weight)	30 (48)	50 (80)	60 (96)	70[†] (112)
Goods vehicles (exceeding 7.5 tonnes maximum laden weight)	30 (48)	40 (64)	50 (80)	60 (96)

*The 30 mph limit usually applies to all traffic on all roads with street lighting unless signs show otherwise
[†] 60 mph (96 km/h) if articulated or towing a trailer.

General rules, techniques and advice for all drivers and riders

Speed limits

124 You **MUST NOT** exceed the maximum speed limits for the road and for your vehicle (see the table on page 40). The presence of street lights generally means that there is a 30 mph (48 km/h) speed limit unless otherwise specified.

Laws RTRO Arts 36, 39 & 43, & MV(SL)R

125 The speed limit is the absolute maximum and does not mean that it is safe to drive at that speed irrespective of the conditions. Driving at speeds too fast for the road and driving conditions can be dangerous. You should always reduce your speed when

- the road layout or condition presents hazards such as bends
- sharing the road with pedestrians, cyclists and horse riders, particularly children and motorcyclists
- weather conditions make it safer to do so
- driving at night, as it is more difficult to see other road users.

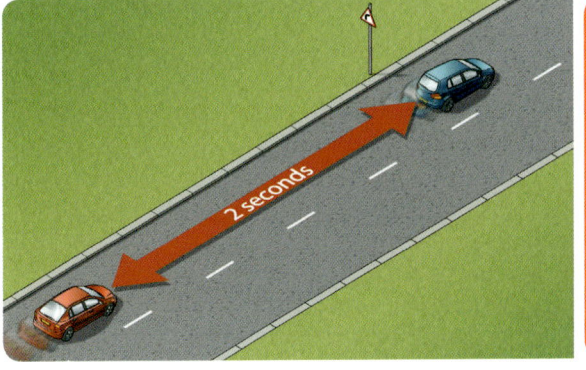

Rule 126 Use a fixed point to help measure a two-second gap

126 **Stopping distances**. Drive at a speed that will allow you to stop well within the distance you can see to be clear. You should

- leave enough space between you and the vehicle in front so that you can pull up safely if it suddenly slows down or stops. The safe rule is to never get closer than

Typical stopping distances

20 mph
(32 km/h) — 6 m + 6 m = **12 metres (40 feet)** or three car lengths

30 mph
(48 km/h) — 9 m + 14 m = **23 metres (75 feet)** or six car lengths

40 mph
(64 km/h) — 12 m + 24 m = **36 metres (118 feet)** or nine car lengths

50 mph
(80 km/h) — 15 m + 38 m

60 mph
(96 km/h) — 18 m + 55 m

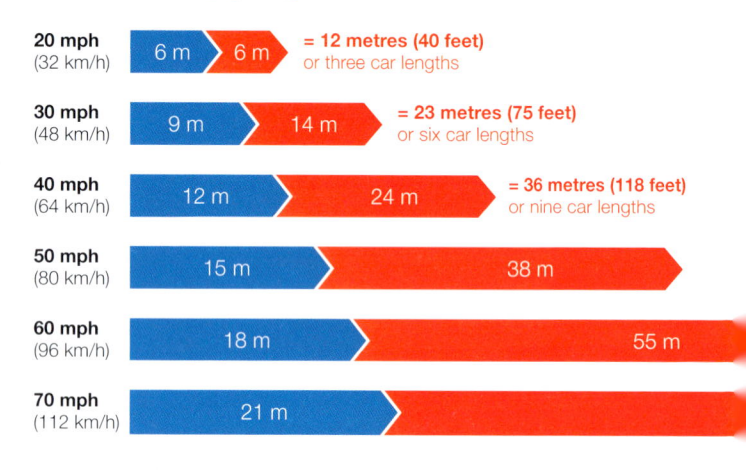

70 mph
(112 km/h) — 21 m

the overall stopping distance (see the Typical Stopping Distances diagram shown above)

- allow at least a two-second gap between you and the vehicle in front on roads carrying fast-moving traffic and in tunnels where visibility is reduced. The gap should be at least doubled on wet roads and increased still further on icy roads

- remember large vehicles and motorcycles need a greater distance to stop. If driving a large vehicle in a tunnel, you should allow a four-second gap between you and the vehicle in front.

If you have to stop in a tunnel, leave at least a 5-metre gap between you and the vehicle in front.

What parts of your vehicle must you keep clear of snow?

Turn to rule 229 (page 77)

General rules, techniques and advice for all drivers and riders

The distances shown are a general guide. The distance will depend on your attention (thinking distance), the road surface, the weather conditions and the condition of your vehicle at the time.

| Thinking Distance | Braking Distance |

Average car length = 4 metres (13 feet)

= 53 metres (175 feet)
or thirteen car lengths

= 73 metres (240 feet)
or eighteen car lengths

75 m
= 96 metres (315 feet)
or twenty-four car lengths

Lines and lane markings on the road

Diagrams of all lines are shown on page 114.

127 **A broken white line.** This marks the centre of the road. When this line lengthens and the gaps shorten, it means that there is a hazard ahead. Do not cross it unless you can see the road is clear and wish to overtake or turn off.

128 **Double white lines where the line nearer to you is broken.** This means you may cross the lines to overtake if it is safe, provided you can complete the manoeuvre before reaching a solid white line on your side. White direction arrows on the road indicate that you need to get back onto your side of the road.

129 **Double white lines where the line nearer you is solid.** This means you **MUST NOT** cross or straddle it unless it is safe and you need to enter adjoining premises or a side road. You may cross the line if necessary, provided the road is clear, to pass a stationary vehicle, or overtake a pedal cycle, horse or road maintenance vehicle, if they are travelling at 10 mph (16 km/h) or less.

Laws RTO 1995 Art 50 & TSR reg 25

130 **Areas of white diagonal stripes** or chevrons painted on the road. These are to separate traffic lanes or to protect traffic turning right.

- If the area is bordered by a broken white line, you should not enter the area unless it is necessary and you can see that it is safe to do so
- If the area is marked by chevrons and bordered by solid white lines, you **MUST NOT** enter it, except in an emergency

Laws RTO 1995 Art 50 & TSR reg 8

131 **Lane dividers**. These are short broken white lines which are used on wide carriageways to divide them into lanes. You should keep between them.

Rule 132 Reflective road studs mark the lanes and edges of the carriageway

132 **Reflective road studs** may be used with white lines

- White studs mark the lanes or the middle of the road
- Red studs mark the left edge of the road
- Amber studs mark the central reservation of a dual carriageway or motorway.
- Green studs mark the edge of the main carriageway at lay-bys and slip roads
- Green/yellow studs indicate temporary adjustments to lane layouts e.g. where road works are taking place.

Multi-lane carriageways

Lane discipline

133 If you need to change lane, first use your mirrors and if necessary take a quick sideways glance to make sure you will not force another road user to change course or speed. When it safe to do so, signal to indicate your intentions to other road users and when clear move over.

134 You should follow the signs and road markings and get into the lane as directed. In congested road conditions do not change lanes unnecessarily. Merging in turn is recommended but only safe and appropriate when vehicles are travelling at very low speed, e.g. when approaching road works or a road traffic incident. It is not recommended at high speed.

Single carriageway

135 Where a single carriageway has three lanes and the road markings or signs do not give priority to traffic in either direction

- use the middle lane only for overtaking or turning right. Remember, you have no more right to use the middle lane than a driver coming from the opposite direction

- do not use the right-hand lane.

136 Where a single carriageway has four or more lanes, use only the lanes that signs or markings indicate.

Dual carriageways

A dual carriageway is a road which has a central reservation to separate the carriageways.

137 On a two-lane dual carriageway you should stay in the left-hand lane. Use the right-hand lane for overtaking or turning right. After overtaking, move back to the left-hand lane when it is safe to do so.

138 On a three-lane dual carriageway, you may use the middle lane or the right-hand lane to overtake but return to the middle and then the left-hand lane when it is safe.

139 **Climbing and crawler lanes**. These are provided on some hills. Use this lane if you are driving a slow-moving vehicle or if there are vehicles behind you wishing to overtake. Be aware of the signs and markings which indicate the lane is about to end.

140 **Cycle lanes**. These are shown by road markings and signs. You **MUST NOT** drive or park in a cycle lane marked by a solid white line during its time of operation. Do not drive or park in a cycle lane marked by a broken white line unless it is unavoidable. You **MUST NOT** park in any cycle lane whilst waiting restrictions apply.

Law RTRO Art 4(5)

141 **Bus lanes**. These are shown by road markings and signs that indicate which (if any) other vehicles are permitted to use the bus lane, and the times of operation. Unless otherwise indicated, you **MUST NOT** drive or ride in a bus lane during its period of operation.

Law RTRO Art 4(1, 2 & 3)

142 **High occupancy vehicle lanes (Great Britain only) and other designated vehicle lanes**. Lanes may be restricted for use by particular types of vehicle; these restrictions may apply some or all of the time. The operating times and vehicle types will be indicated on the accompanying traffic signs. You **MUST NOT** drive in such lanes during their times of operation unless signs indicate your vehicle is permitted. (see page 112).

Vehicles permitted to use designated lanes may or may not include cycles, buses, taxis, licensed private hire vehicles, motorcycles, heavy goods vehicles (HGVs), and high occupancy vehicles (HOVs).

General rules, techniques and advice for all drivers and riders

Where HOV lanes are in operation, they **MUST** only be used by

- vehicles containing at least the minimum number of people indicated on the traffic signs
- any other vehicles, such as buses and motorcycles, as indicated on signs prior to the start of the lane, irrespective of the number of occupants.

Law RTRO Art 4(5)

143 **One-way streets**. Traffic **MUST** travel in the direction indicated by signs. Buses and/or cycles may have a contraflow lane. Choose the correct lane for your exit as soon as you can. Do not change lanes suddenly. Unless road signs or markings indicate otherwise, you should use

- the left-hand lane when going left
- the right-hand lane when going right
- the most appropriate lane when going straight ahead.

Remember, traffic could be passing on both sides.

Laws RTO 1995 Art 50 & RTRO Arts 4(5) & 5(9)

General advice

144 You **MUST NOT**

- drive dangerously
- drive without due care and attention
- drive without reasonable consideration for other road users.

Law RTO 1995 Arts 10 & 12

145 You **MUST NOT** drive on or over a footway or footpath except to gain lawful access to property, or in the case of an emergency.

Law RTRO Art 3

146 **Adapt your driving** to the appropriate type and condition of the road you are on. In particular

- do not treat speed limits as a target. It is often not appropriate or safe to drive at the maximum speed limit

- take the road and traffic conditions into account. Be prepared for unexpected or difficult situations, for example the road being blocked beyond a blind bend. Be prepared to adjust your speed as a precaution

- where there are junctions, be prepared for road users emerging

- in side roads and country lanes look out for unmarked junctions where nobody has priority

- be prepared to stop at traffic control systems, road works, pedestrian crossings or traffic lights as necessary

- try to anticipate what cyclists or pedestrians might do. If pedestrians, particularly children, are looking the other way, they may step out into the road without seeing you.

147 **Be considerate**. Be careful and considerate towards other road users, especially those requiring extra care (see Rule 204).

- You **MUST NOT** throw anything out of a vehicle; for example, food or food packaging, cigarette ends, cans, paper or carrier bags. This can endanger other road users, particularly motorcyclists and cyclists.

- Try to be understanding if other road users cause problems; they may be inexperienced or not know the area well.

- Be patient; remember that anyone can make a mistake.

- Do not allow yourself to become agitated or involved if someone is behaving badly on the road. This will only make the situation worse. Pull over, calm down and, when you feel relaxed, continue your journey.

- Slow down and hold back if a road user pulls out into your path at a junction. Allow them to get clear. Do not over-react by driving too close behind to intimidate them.

Law LO

General rules, techniques and advice for all drivers and riders

148 **Safe driving and riding needs concentration.** Avoid distractions when driving such as

- loud music (this may mask other sounds)
- trying to read maps
- starting or adjusting any music or radio
- arguing with your passengers or other road users
- eating and drinking
- smoking

You **MUST NOT** smoke in public transport vehicles or in vehicles used for work purposes in certain prescribed circumstances.

Laws SO & SF(EVPDA)R reg 12(1)

Mobile phones and in-vehicle technology

149 You **MUST** exercise proper control of your vehicle at all times. You **MUST NOT** use a hand-held mobile phone, or similar device, when driving or when supervising a learner driver, except to call 999 or 112 in a genuine emergency when it is unsafe or impractical to stop. Never use a hand-held microphone when driving. Using hands-free equipment is also likely to distract your attention from the road. It is far safer not to use any telephone while you are driving or riding - find a safe place to stop first or use the voicemail facility and listen to messages later.

Laws RTO 1995 Arts 10, 12 & 56A, & CUR regs 120 & 125A

150 There is a danger of driver distraction being caused by in-vehicle systems such as satellite navigation systems, congestion warning systems, PCs, multimedia, etc. You **MUST** exercise proper control of your vehicle at all times. Do not rely on driver assistance programs such as cruise control or lane departure warnings. They are available to assist but you should not reduce your concentration levels. Do not be distracted by maps or screen-based information (such as navigation or vehicle management systems) while driving or riding. If necessary find a safe place to stop.

Laws RTO 1995 Arts 10 & 12, & CUR reg 120

Rule 151
Do not block access to a side road

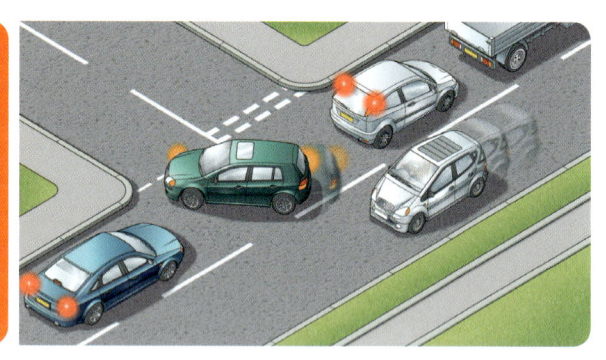

151 **In slow-moving traffic.** You should

- reduce the distance between you and the vehicle ahead to maintain traffic flow

- never get so close to the vehicle in front that you cannot stop safely

- leave enough space to be able to manoeuvre if the vehicle in front breaks down or an emergency vehicle needs to get past

- not change lanes to the left to overtake

- allow access into and from side roads, as blocking these will add to congestion

- be aware of cyclists and motorcyclists who may be passing on either side.

Driving in built-up areas

152 **Residential streets.** You should drive slowly and carefully on streets where there are likely to be pedestrians, cyclists and parked vehicles. In some areas a 20 mph (32 km/h) maximum speed limit may be in force. Look out for

- vehicles emerging from junctions or driveways
- vehicles moving off
- vehicle doors opening
- pedestrians
- children running out from between parked vehicles
- cyclists and motorcyclists.

General rules, techniques and advice for all drivers and riders

153 **Traffic calming measures.** On some roads there are features such as road humps, chicanes and narrowings which are intended to slow you down. When you approach these features reduce your speed. Allow cyclists and motorcyclists room to pass through them. Maintain a reduced speed along the whole of the stretch of road within the calming measures. Give way to oncoming road users if directed to do so by signs. You should not overtake other moving road users while in these areas.

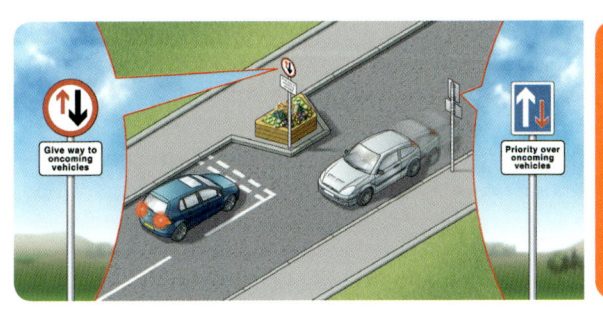

Rule 153 Chicanes may be used to slow traffic down

Country roads

154 Take extra care on country roads and reduce your speed at approaches to bends, which can be sharper than they appear, and at junctions and turnings, which may be partially hidden. Be prepared for pedestrians, horse riders, cyclists, slow moving farm vehicles or mud on the road surface. Make sure you can stop within the distance you can see to be clear. You should also reduce your speed where country roads enter villages.

When can you use a mobile phone in your car?

Turn to rule 149 (page 49)

155 Single-track roads. These are only wide enough for one vehicle. They may have special passing places. If you see a vehicle coming towards you, or the driver behind wants to overtake, pull into a passing place on your left, or wait opposite a passing place on your right. Give way to road users coming up hill whenever you can. If necessary reverse until you reach a passing place to let the other road user pass. Slow down when passing pedestrians, cyclists and horse riders.

156 Do not park in passing places.

Vehicles prohibited from using roads, footways and footpaths

157 Certain motorised vehicles do not meet the construction and technical requirements for road vehicles and are generally not intended, not suitable and not legal for road, footway, footpath or cycle path use. These include most types of miniature motorcycles, also called mini motos, and motorised scooters also called gopeds, which are powered by electric or internal combustion engines. These types of vehicles **MUST NOT** be used on roads, footways or footpaths.

Law RTO 1995 Arts 48, 56, 58, 63 & 72

158 Certain models of motorcycles, motor tricycles and quadricycles, also called quad bikes, are suitable only for off-road use and do not meet the legal standards for use on roads. Vehicles that do not meet these standards **MUST NOT** be used on roads. They **MUST NOT** be used on footways, footpaths or cycle paths either. You **MUST** make sure that any motorcycle, motor tricycle, quadricycles or any other motor vehicle meets legal standards and is properly registered, taxed and insured before using it on the roads. Even when registered, taxed and insured for the road, vehicles **MUST NOT** be used on footways or footpaths.

Laws RTO 1995 Arts 48, 56, 63 & 72, & VERA sects 1, 29, 31A & 43A

Using the road

General rules

159 Before moving off you should

- use all mirrors to check the road is clear
- look round to check the blind spots (the areas you are unable to see in the mirrors)
- signal if necessary before moving out
- look round for a final check.

Move off only when it is safe to do so.

Rule 159 Check the blind spot before moving off

160 **Once moving** you should

- keep to the left, unless road signs or markings indicate otherwise. The exceptions are when you want to overtake, turn right or pass parked vehicles or pedestrians in the road
- keep well to the left on right-hand bends. This will improve your view of the road and help avoid the risk of colliding with traffic approaching from the opposite direction
- drive or ride with both hands on the wheel or handlebars, where possible. This will help you to remain in full control of the vehicle at all times

- be aware of other vehicles especially cycles and motorcycles that may be filtering through traffic. These are more difficult to see than larger vehicles and their riders are particularly vulnerable. Give them plenty of room especially if you are driving a long vehicle or towing a trailer
- select a lower gear before you reach a long downhill slope. This will help to control your speed
- when towing, remember the extra length will affect overtaking and manoeuvring. The extra weight will also affect the braking and acceleration.

161 **Mirrors.** All mirrors should be used effectively throughout your journey. You should

- use your mirrors frequently so that you always know what is behind and to each side of you
- use them in good time before you signal or change direction or speed
- be aware that mirrors do not cover all areas and that there will be blind spots. You will need to look round and check.

Remember: Mirrors–Signal–Manoeuvre

Overtaking

162 **Before overtaking** you should make sure

- the road is sufficiently clear ahead
- road users are not beginning to overtake you
- there is a suitable gap in front of the road user you plan to overtake.

163 **Overtake only** when it is safe and legal to do so. You should

- not get too close to the vehicle you intend to overtake
- use your mirrors, signal when it is safe to do so, take a quick sideways glance if necessary into the blind spot area and then start to move out

Using the road

- not assume you can simply follow a vehicle ahead which is overtaking; there may only be enough room for one vehicle
- move quickly past the vehicle you are overtaking, once you have started to overtake. Allow plenty of room. Move back to the left as soon as you can but do not cut in

Rule 163
Give vulnerable road users at least as much space as you would a car

- take extra care at night and in poor visibility when it is harder to judge speed and distance
- give way to oncoming vehicles before passing parked vehicles or other obstructions on your side of the road
- only overtake on the left if the vehicle in front is signalling to turn right, and there is room to do so
- stay in your lane if traffic is moving slowly in queues. If the queue on your right is moving more slowly than you are, you may pass on the left
- give motorcyclists, cyclists and horse riders at least as much room as you would when overtaking a car (see Rules 211–215).

Remember: Mirrors–Signal–Manoeuvre

164 **Large vehicles.** Overtaking these is more difficult. You should

- drop back. This will increase your ability to see ahead and should allow the drivers of large vehicles to see you in their mirrors. Getting too close to large vehicles, including agricultural vehicles such as a tractor with a trailer or other fixed equipment, will obscure your view of the road ahead and there may be another slow moving vehicle in front

Rule 164 Do not cut in too quickly

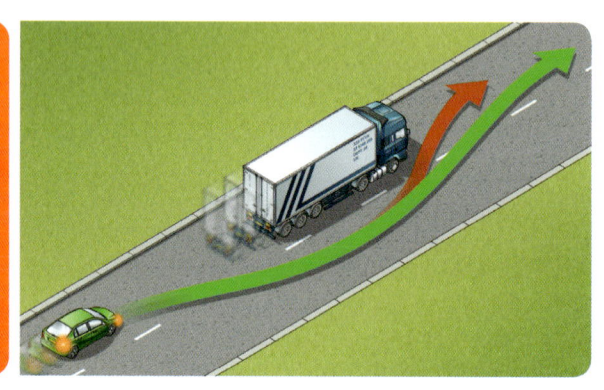

- make sure that you have enough room to complete your overtaking manoeuvre before committing yourself. It takes longer to pass a large vehicle. If in doubt, do not overtake

- not assume you can follow a vehicle ahead which is overtaking a long vehicle. If a problem develops, they may abort overtaking and pull back in.

165 You **MUST NOT** overtake

- if you have to cross or straddle double white lines with a solid line nearest to you (but see Rule 129)

- if you would have to enter an area designed to divide traffic, if it is surrounded by a solid white line

- the nearest vehicle to a signal-controlled crossing facility, especially when it has stopped to let pedestrians, equestrian traffic or cyclists to cross

Using the road

- if you would have to enter a lane reserved for buses, trams or cycles during its hours of operation
- after a 'No Overtaking' sign and until you pass a sign cancelling the restriction.

Laws RTO 1995 Art 50, TSR regs 8, 25 & 25B, RTRO Art 59(4) & PCR reg 20

166 **DO NOT** overtake if there is any doubt, or where you cannot see far enough ahead to be sure it is safe. For example when you are approaching

- a corner or a bend
- a hump bridge
- the brow of a hill.

167 **DO NOT** overtake where you might come into conflict with other road users. For example

- approaching or at a road junction on either side of the road
- where the road narrows
- when approaching a school crossing patrol
- between a kerb and a bus or tram when it is at a stop
- where traffic is queuing at junctions or road works
- when you would force another road user to swerve or slow down
- at a level crossing
- when a road user is indicating right, even if you believe the signal should have been cancelled. Do not take a risk; wait for the signal to be cancelled.
- stay behind if you are following a cyclist approaching a roundabout or junction, and you intend to turn left
- when a tram is standing at a kerbside tram stop and there is no clearly marked passing lane for other traffic.

168 **Being overtaken.** If a driver is trying to overtake you, maintain a steady course and speed, slowing down if necessary to let the vehicle pass. Never obstruct drivers who wish to pass. Speeding up or driving unpredictably when someone is overtaking you is dangerous. Drop back to maintain a two-second gap if someone overtakes and pulls into the gap in front of you.

169 Do not hold up a long queue of traffic, especially if you are driving a large or slow-moving vehicle. Check your mirrors frequently, and if necessary, pull in where it is safe and let traffic pass.

Road junctions

170 Take extra care at junctions. You should

- watch out for cyclists, motorcyclists, powered wheelchairs/mobility scooters and pedestrians as they are not always easy to see. Be aware that they may not have seen or heard you if you are approaching from behind

- watch out for pedestrians crossing a road into which you are turning. If they have started to cross they have priority, so give way

- watch out for long vehicles which may be turning at a junction ahead; they may have to use the whole width of the road to make the turn (see Rule 221)

Rule 170 Give way to pedestrians who have started to cross

Using the road

- watch out for horse riders who may take a different line on the road from that which you would expect
- not assume, when waiting at a junction, that a vehicle coming from the right and signalling left will actually turn. Wait and make sure
- look all around before emerging. Do not cross or join a road until there is a gap large enough for you to do so safely.

171 You **MUST** stop behind a line at a junction with a 'Stop' sign and a solid white line across the road. Wait for a safe gap in the traffic before you move off.

Laws RTO 1995 Art 50 & TSR regs 8 & 14

172 The approach to a junction may have a 'Give Way' sign or a triangle marked on the road. You **MUST** give way to traffic on the main road when emerging from a junction with broken white lines across the road.

Laws RTO 1995 Art 50 & TSR regs 8, 14 & 24

Rule 173 Assess your vehicle's length and do not obstruct traffic

173 **Dual carriageways**. When crossing, or turning right, first assess whether the central reservation is deep enough to protect the full length of your vehicle.

- If it is, then you should treat each half of the carriageway as a separate road. Wait in the central reservation until there is a safe gap in the traffic on the second half of the road.

- If the central reservation is too shallow for the length of your vehicle, wait until you can cross both carriageways in one go.

Rule 174 Enter a box junction only if your exit road is clear

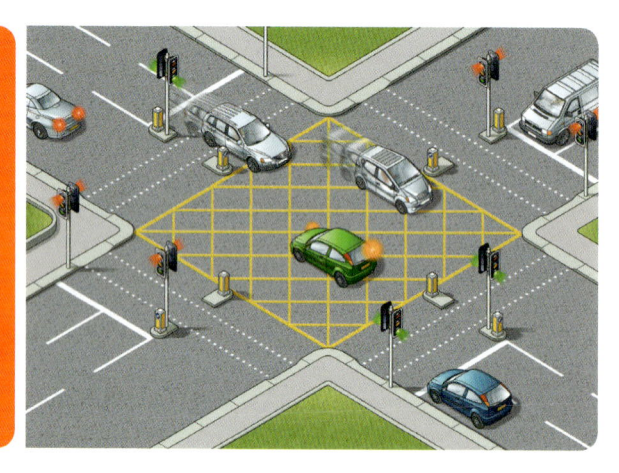

174 **Box junctions**. These have criss-cross yellow lines painted on the road (see page 116). You **MUST NOT** enter the box until your exit road or lane is clear. However, you may enter the box and wait when you want to turn right, and are only stopped from doing so by oncoming traffic, or by other vehicles waiting to turn right. At signalled roundabouts you **MUST NOT** enter the box unless you can cross over it completely without stopping.

Laws RTO 1995 Art 50 & TSR regs 8 & 26

Junctions controlled by traffic lights

175 You **MUST** stop behind the white 'Stop' line across your side of the road unless the light is green. If the amber light appears you may go on only if you have already crossed the stop line or are so close to it that to stop might cause a collision.

Laws RTO 1995 Art 50 & TSR regs 8 & 33

Using the road

176 You **MUST NOT** move forward over the white line when the red light is showing. Only go forward when the traffic lights are green if there is room for you to clear the junction safely or you are taking up a position to turn right. If the traffic lights are not working, treat the situation as you would an unmarked junction and proceed with great care.

Laws RTO 1995 Art 50 & TSR regs 8 & 33

177 **Green filter arrow**. This indicates a filter lane only. Do not enter that lane unless you want to go in the direction of the arrow. You may proceed in the direction of the green arrow when it, or the full green light, shows. Give other traffic, especially cyclists, time and room to move into the correct lane.

Rule 178
Do not unnecessarily encroach on the cyclists' waiting area

178 **Advanced stop lines**. Some signal-controlled junctions have advanced stop lines to allow cycles to be positioned ahead of other traffic. Motorists, including motorcyclists, **MUST** stop at the first white line reached, and should avoid blocking the way or encroaching on the marked area at other times e.g. if the junction ahead is blocked. If your vehicle has proceeded over the first white line at the time that the signal goes red, you **MUST** stop at the second white line, even if your vehicle is in the marked area. Allow cyclists time and space to move off when the green signal shows.

Laws RTO 1995 Art 50(1) & TSR reg 33(6)

Turning right

179 **Well before** you turn right you should

- use your mirrors to make sure you know the position and movement of traffic behind you
- give a right-turn signal
- take up a position just left of the middle of the road or in the space for traffic turning right
- leave room for other vehicles to pass on the left, if possible.

180 Wait until there is a safe gap between you and any oncoming vehicle. Watch out for cyclists, motorcyclists, pedestrians and other road users. Check your mirrors and blind spots again to make sure you are not being overtaken, then make the turn.

Do not cut the corner. Take great care when turning into a main road; you will need to watch for traffic in both directions and wait for a safe gap.

Remember: Mirrors–Signal–Manoeuvre

Rule 180 Position your vehicle correctly to avoid obstructing traffic

181 **When turning** right at a cross roads where an oncoming vehicle is also turning right, there is a choice of two methods

- turn right side to right side; keep the other vehicle on your right and turn behind it. This is generally the safer method as you have a clear view of any approaching traffic when completing your turn

62

- left side to left side, turning in front of each other. This can block your view of oncoming vehicles, so take extra care. Cyclists and motorcyclists in particular may be hidden from your view.

Road layout, markings or how the other vehicle is positioned can determine which course should be taken.

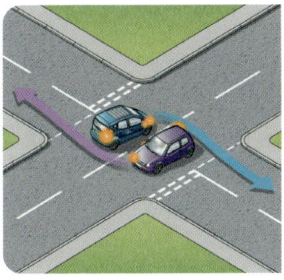

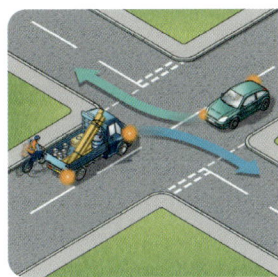

Rule 181
Left – Turning right side to right side.
Right – Turning left side to left side

Turning left

182 Use your mirrors and give a left-turn signal well before you turn left. Do not overtake just as you turn left and watch out for traffic coming up on your left before you make the turn, especially if driving a large vehicle. Cyclists and motorcyclists in particular may be hidden from your view.

Rule 182
Do not cut in on cyclists

183 When turning

- keep as close to the left as is safe and practicable
- give way to any vehicles using a bus lane, cycle lane or tramway from either direction.

Roundabouts

184 **On approaching a roundabout** take notice and act on all the information available to you, including traffic signs, traffic lights and lane markings which direct you into the correct lane. You should

- use **Mirrors – Signal – Manoeuvre** at all stages
- decide as early as possible which exit you need to take
- give an appropriate signal (see Rule 186). Time your signals so as not to confuse other road users
- get into the correct lane
- adjust your speed and position to fit in with traffic conditions
- be aware of the speed and position of all the road users around you.

185 **When reaching the roundabout** you should

- give priority to traffic approaching from your right unless directed otherwise by signs, road markings or traffic lights
- check whether road markings allow you to enter the roundabout without giving way. If so, proceed, but still look to the right before joining
- watch out for all other road users already on the roundabout; be aware they may not be signalling correctly or at all
- look forward before moving off to make sure traffic in front has moved off.

Rule 185 Position your vehicle correctly to avoid obstructing traffic

Using the road

186 **Signals and position.**
When taking the first exit to the left, unless signs or markings indicate otherwise

- signal left and approach in the left hand lane
- keep to the left on the roundabout and continue signalling left to leave.

When taking an exit to the right or going full circle, unless signs or markings indicate otherwise

- signal right and approach in the right-hand lane
- keep to the right on the roundabout until you need to change lanes to exit the roundabout
- signal left after you have passed the exit before the one you want.

When taking any intermediate exit, unless signs or markings indicate otherwise

- select the appropriate lane on approach to the roundabout
- you should not normally need to signal on approach
- stay in this lane until you need to alter course to exit the roundabout
- signal left after you have passed the exit before the one you want.

When there are more than three lanes at the entrance to a roundabout, use the most appropriate lane on approach and through it.

For more specific advice on procedures at roundabouts, see Appendix on pages 136–140.

187 **In all cases watch out for** and give plenty of room to

- pedestrians who may be crossing the approach and exit roads
- traffic crossing in front of you on the roundabout, especially vehicles intending to leave by the next exit
- traffic which may be straddling lanes or positioned incorrectly
- motorcyclists

- cyclists and horse riders who may stay in the left-hand lane and signal right if they intend to continue around the roundabout. Allow them to do so
- long vehicles (including those towing trailers). These might have to take a different course or straddle lanes either approaching or on the roundabout because of their length. Watch out for their signals.

188 **Mini-roundabouts**. Approach these in the same way as normal roundabouts. All vehicles **MUST** pass round the central markings except large vehicles which are physically incapable of doing so. Remember, there is less space to manoeuvre and less time to signal. Avoid making U-turns at mini-roundabouts. Beware of others doing this.

Laws RTO 1995 Art 50 & TSR regs 8 & 14

189 At double mini-roundabouts treat each roundabout separately and give way to traffic from the right.

190 **Multiple roundabouts**. At some complex junctions there may be a series of mini-roundabouts at each intersection. Treat each mini-roundabout separately and follow the normal rules.

Rule 190 Treat each roundabout separately

Pedestrian crossings

191 You **MUST NOT** park on a crossing or in the area covered by the zigzag lines. You **MUST NOT** overtake the moving vehicle nearest the crossing or the vehicle nearest the crossing which has stopped to give way to pedestrians.

Laws RTRO Art 59(4) & PCR regs 16, 18 & 20

Using the road

192 In queuing traffic, you should keep the crossing clear.

Rule 192 Keep the crossing clear

193 You should take extra care where the view of either side of the crossing is blocked by queuing traffic or incorrectly parked vehicles. Pedestrians may be crossing between stationary vehicles.

194 Allow pedestrians plenty of time to cross and do not harass them by revving your engine or edging forward.

195 **Zebra crossings**. As you approach a zebra crossing

- look out for people waiting to cross and be ready to slow down or stop to let them cross
- you **MUST** give way when a pedestrian has moved onto a crossing
- allow more time for stopping on wet or icy roads
- do not wave or use your horn to invite pedestrians across; this could be dangerous if another vehicle is approaching
- be aware of pedestrians approaching from the side of the crossing.

A zebra crossing with a central island is two separate crossings (see picture on page 10).

Laws RTRO Art 59(4) & PCR reg 21

Signal-controlled crossings

196 **Pelican crossings**. These are signal-controlled crossings where flashing amber follows the red 'Stop' light. You **MUST** stop when the red light shows. When the amber light is flashing, you **MUST** give way to any pedestrians on the crossing. If the amber light is flashing and there are no pedestrians on the crossing, you may proceed with caution.

Laws RTRO Art 59(4) & PCR regs 10, 19 & 22

197 Pelican crossings which go straight across the road are one crossing, even when there is a central island. You **MUST** wait for pedestrians who are crossing from the other side of the island.

Laws RTRO Art 59(4) & PCR reg 22

198 Give way to anyone still crossing after the signal for vehicles has changed to green. This advice applies to all crossings.

199 **Toucan, puffin and equestrian crossings**. These are similar to pelican crossings, but there is no flashing amber phase; the light sequence for traffic at these three crossings is the same as at traffic lights. If the signal-controlled crossing is not working, proceed with extreme caution.

Rule 199 There is no flashing amber phase at a puffin crossing

Reversing

200 Choose an appropriate place to manoeuvre. If you need to turn your vehicle around, wait until you find a safe place. Try not to reverse or turn around in a busy road; find a quiet side road or drive round a block of side streets.

Using the road

201 Do not reverse from a side road into a main road. When using a driveway, reverse in and drive out if you can.

202 Look carefully before you start reversing. You should

- use all your mirrors
- check any 'blind spot' behind you (the part of the road you cannot see easily in the mirrors)
- check there are no pedestrians (particularly children), cyclists, other road users or obstructions in the road behind you.

Rule 202 Check all round when reversing

Reverse slowly while

- checking all around
- looking mainly through the rear window
- being aware that the front of your vehicle will swing out as you turn.

Get someone to guide you if you cannot see clearly.

203 You **MUST NOT** reverse your vehicle further than necessary.

Law CUR reg 122

Road users requiring extra care

204 The most vulnerable road users are pedestrians, cyclists, motorcyclists and horse riders. It is particularly important to be aware of children, elderly and disabled people, and learner and inexperienced drivers and riders.

Pedestrians

205 There is a risk of pedestrians, especially children, stepping unexpectedly into the road. You should drive with the safety of children in mind at a speed suitable for the conditions.

206 **Drive carefully and slowly** when

- in crowded shopping streets, Home Zones and Quiet Lanes (see Rule 218) or residential areas
- driving past bus and tram stops; pedestrians may emerge suddenly into the road
- passing parked vehicles, especially ice-cream vans; children are more interested in ice-cream than traffic and may run into the road unexpectedly
- needing to cross a footway, footpath, cycle lane or cycle track; for example to reach or leave a driveway. Give way to pedestrians on the footway or footpath and to cyclists on the cycle lane or cycle track
- reversing into a side road; look all around the vehicle and give way to any pedestrians who are already crossing the road into which you are turning
- the footway or footpath is closed due to street repairs and pedestrians are directed to use the road
- approaching pedestrians on narrow rural roads without a footway or footpath. Always slow down and be prepared to stop if necessary, giving them plenty of room as you drive past.

Road users requiring extra care

Rule 206 Watch out for children in busy areas

207 **Particularly vulnerable pedestrians**. These include

- children and older pedestrians who may not be able to judge your speed and could step into the road in front of you. At 40 mph (64 km/h) your vehicle will probably kill any pedestrian it hits. At 20 mph (32 km/h) there is only a 1 in 20 chance of the pedestrian being killed. So kill your speed

- older pedestrians who may need more time to cross the road. Be patient and allow them to cross in their own time. Do not hurry them by revving your engine or edging forward

- people with disabilities. People with hearing impairments may not be aware of your vehicle approaching. Those with walking difficulties require more time

- blind or partially sighted people who may be carrying a white cane or using a guide dog. They may not be able to see you approaching

- deafblind people who may be carrying a white cane with a red band or using a dog with a red and white harness. They may not see or hear instructions or signals.

208 **Near schools**. Drive slowly and be particularly aware of young cyclists and pedestrians. In some places, there may be a flashing amber signal accompanying the 'School' or 'Patrol' warning sign which tells you that there may be children crossing the road ahead. Drive very slowly until you are clear of the area.

209 Drive carefully when passing a stationary bus carrying school children or showing 'School Bus' markings or signs as children may be getting on or off.

210 You **MUST** stop when a school crossing patrol shows a 'Stop for children' sign (see pages 105 and 106).

Law RTRO Art 60

Motorcyclists and cyclists

211 It is often difficult to see motorcyclists and cyclists, especially when they are coming up from behind, coming out of junctions, at roundabouts, overtaking you or filtering through traffic. Always look out for them before you emerge from a junction; they could be approaching faster than you think. When turning right across a line of slow-moving or stationary traffic, look out for cyclists or motorcyclists on the inside of the traffic you are crossing. Be especially careful when turning and when changing direction or lane. Be sure to check mirrors and blind spots carefully.

Rule 211 Look out for motorcyclists and cyclists at junctions

212 When passing motorcyclists and cyclists, give them plenty of room (see rules 162–167). If they look over their shoulder it could mean that they intend to pull out, turn right or change direction. Give them time and space to do so.

Road users requiring extra care

213 Motorcyclists and cyclists may suddenly need to avoid uneven road surfaces and obstacles such as drain covers or oily, wet or icy patches on the road. Give them plenty of room and pay particular attention to any sudden change of direction they may have to make.

Other road users

214 **Animals**. When passing animals, drive slowly. Give them plenty of room and be ready to stop. Do not scare animals by sounding your horn, revving your engine, or accelerating rapidly once you have passed them. Look out for animals being led, driven or ridden on the road and take extra care. Keep your speed down at bends and on narrow country roads. If a road is blocked by a herd of animals, stop and switch off your engine until they have left the road. Watch out for animals on unfenced roads.

215 **Horse riders and horse-drawn vehicles**. Be particularly careful of horses and horse-drawn vehicles especially when overtaking. Always pass wide and slowly. Horse riders are often children, so take extra care and remember riders may ride in double file when escorting a young or inexperienced horse or rider. Look out for horse riders' and horse drivers' signals and heed a request to slow down or stop. Take great care and treat all horses as a potential hazard; they can be unpredictable despite the efforts of their rider/driver.

216 **Older drivers**. Their reactions may be slower than other drivers. Make allowance for this.

217 **Learners and inexperienced drivers**. They may not be so skilful at anticipating and responding to events. Be particularly patient with learner drivers, restricted drivers and young drivers. Drivers are required to display R plates for one year after passing their test, not counting any periods of disqualification or revocation (see Annex 8 – Safety Code for New Drivers).

218 **Home Zones and Quiet Lanes** (Great Britain only). These are places where people could be using the whole of the road for a range of activities such as children playing or for a community event. You should drive slowly and carefully and be prepared to stop or allow people extra time to make space for you to pass them in safety.

Other vehicles

219 **Emergency and incident support vehicles.** You should look and listen for ambulances, fire engines, police, doctors or other emergency vehicles using blue, red or green lights and sirens or flashing headlights or for Driver and Vehicle Agency Enforcement Officer vehicles using flashing amber lights. When one approaches do not panic. Consider the route of such a vehicle and take appropriate action to let it pass, while complying with all the traffic signs. If necessary, pull to the side of the road and stop, but try to avoid stopping before the brow of a hill, a bend or narrow section of road. Do not endanger yourself or other road users and avoid mounting the kerb. Do not brake harshly on approach to a junction or roundabout, as a following vehicle may not have the same view as you.

220 **Powered vehicles used by disabled people.** These small vehicles travel at a maximum speed of 8 mph (12 km/h). On a dual carriageway where the speed limit exceeds 50 mph (80 km/h) they **MUST** have a flashing amber beacon, but on other roads you may not have that advance warning (see Rules 36–46 inclusive).

Law RVLR regs 20(1) & 29

Road users requiring extra care

221 **Large vehicles**. These may need extra road space to turn or to deal with a hazard that you are not able to see. If you are following a large vehicle, such as a bus or articulated lorry, be aware that the driver may not be able to see you in the mirrors. Be prepared to stop and wait if it needs room or time to turn.

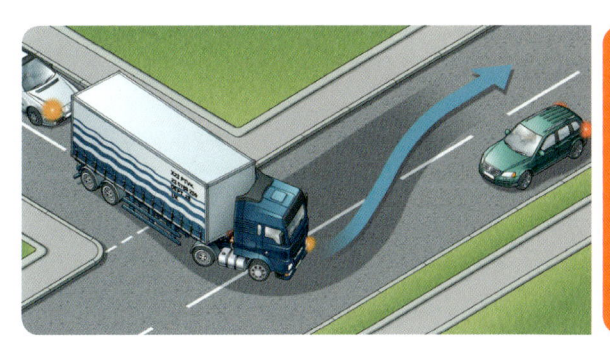

Rule 221 Large vehicles need extra room

222 Large vehicles can block your view. Your ability to see and plan ahead will be improved if you pull back to increase your separation distance. Be patient, as larger vehicles are subject to lower speed limits than cars and motorcycles. Many large vehicles may be fitted with speed limiting devices which will restrict speed to 56 mph (90 km/h) even on a motorway.

223 **Buses, coaches and trams**. Give priority to these vehicles when you can do so safely, especially when they signal to pull away from stops. Look out for people getting off a bus or tram and crossing the road.

224 **Electric vehicles**. Be careful of electric vehicles such as milk floats and trams. Trams move quickly but silently and cannot steer to avoid you.

225 **Vehicles with flashing amber beacons**. These warn of a slow moving or stationary vehicle (such as a Driver and Vehicle Agency vehicle, salt spreader, snow plough or recovery vehicle) or abnormal loads, so approach with caution. On unrestricted dual carriageways, motor vehicles first used on or after 1 January 1947 with a maximum speed of 25 mph (40 km/h) or less (such as tractors) **MUST** use a flashing amber beacon. (Also see Rule 220.)

Law RVLR reg 20

Driving in adverse weather conditions

226 You **MUST** use headlights when visibility is seriously reduced, generally when you cannot see for more than 100 metres (328 feet). You may also use front or rear fog lights but you **MUST** switch them off when visibility improves (see Rule 236).

Law RVLR regs 28 & 30

227 **Wet weather.** In wet weather, stopping distances will be at least double those required for stopping on dry roads (see pages 42–43). This is because your tyres have less grip on the road. In wet weather

- you should keep well back from the vehicle in front. This will increase your ability to see and plan ahead
- if the steering becomes unresponsive, it probably means that water is preventing the tyres from gripping the road. Ease off the accelerator and slow down gradually
- the rain and spray from vehicles may make it difficult to see and be seen
- be aware of the dangers of spilt diesel that will make the surface very slippery (see Annex 6)
- take extra care around pedestrians, cyclists, motorcyclists and horse riders.

Icy and snowy weather

228 In winter check the local weather forecast for warnings of icy or snowy weather. DO NOT drive in these conditions unless your journey is essential. If it is, take great care and allow more time for your journey. Take an emergency kit of de-icer, ice scraper, torch, warm clothing and boots,

Driving in adverse weather conditions

first aid kit, jump leads and a shovel together with a warm drink and emergency food in case you get stuck or your vehicle breaks down.

229 Before you set off

- you **MUST** be able to see, so clear all snow and ice from your windows
- you **MUST** ensure that lights are clean and number plates are clearly visible and legible
- make sure the mirrors are clear and windows are de-misted thoroughly
- remove all snow that might fall into the path of other road users
- check your planned route is clear of delays and that no further snowfall or severe weather are predicted.

Laws CUR reg 35, RVLR reg 26, VERA sect 43 & RV(DRM)R reg 11

Rule 229 Make sure your windscreen is completely clear

230 **When driving** in icy or snowy weather

- drive with care, even if the roads have been treated
- keep well back from the road user in front as stopping distances can be ten times greater than on dry roads

- take care when overtaking vehicles spreading salt or other de-icer, particularly if you are riding a motorcycle or cycle

- watch out for snowploughs which may throw out snow on either side. Do not overtake them unless the lane you intend to take has been cleared

- be prepared for the road conditions to change over relatively short distances

- listen to travel bulletins and take note of variable message signs that may provide information about weather, road and traffic conditions ahead.

231 **Drive extremely carefully** when the roads are icy. Avoid sudden distractions as these could cause loss of control. You should

- drive at a slow speed in as high a gear as possible; accelerate and brake very gently

- drive particularly slowly on bends where loss of control is more likely. Brake progressively on the straight before you reach a bend. Having slowed down, steer smoothly round the bend, avoiding sudden actions

- check your grip on the road surface when there is snow or ice by choosing a safe place to brake gently. If the steering feels unresponsive this may indicate ice and your vehicle losing its grip on the road. When travelling on ice, tyres make virtually no noise.

Windy weather

232 High-sided vehicles are most affected by windy weather, but strong gusts can also blow a car, cyclist, motorcyclist or horse rider off course. This can happen on open stretches of road exposed to strong side winds, or when passing bridges or gaps in the hedges.

233 In very windy weather your vehicle may be affected by turbulence created by large vehicles. Motorcyclists are particularly affected, so keep well back from them when they are overtaking a high-sided vehicle.

Driving in adverse weather conditions

Fog

234 **Before entering fog** check your mirrors then slow down. If the word 'Fog' is shown on a roadside signal or overhead gantry but the road is clear, be prepared for a bank of fog or drifting patchy fog ahead. Even if it seems to be clearing, you can suddenly find yourself in thick fog.

235 **When driving in fog** you should

- use your lights as required (see Rule 226)
- keep a safe distance behind the vehicle in front. Rear lights can give a false sense of security
- be able to pull up well within the distance you can see clearly. This is particularly important on motorways and dual carriageways, as vehicles are travelling faster
- use your windscreen wipers and demisters
- beware of other drivers not using headlights
- not accelerate to get away from a vehicle which is too close behind you.
- check your mirrors before you slow down. Then use your brakes so that your brake lights warn drivers behind you that you are slowing down
- stop in the correct position at a junction with limited visibility and listen for traffic. When you are sure it is safe to emerge do so positively and do not hesitate in a position that puts you directly in the path of approaching vehicles.

236 You **MUST NOT** use front or rear fog lights unless visibility is seriously reduced (see Rule 226), as they dazzle other road users and can obscure your brake lights. You **MUST** switch them off when visibility improves.

Law RVLR regs 28 & 30

Hot weather

237 Keep your vehicle well ventilated to avoid drowsiness. Be aware that the road surface may become soft or if it rains after a dry spell it may become slippery. These conditions could affect your steering and braking. If you are dazzled by bright sunlight, slow down and if necessary stop.

Waiting and parking

238 You **MUST NOT** wait or park on yellow lines, during the times of operation shown on the nearby time plates (or zone entry sign if in a Controlled Parking Zone see pages 112 and 115). Double yellow lines indicate a prohibition of waiting at any time even if there are no upright signs. You **MUST NOT** wait or park, or stop to set down and pick up passengers, on school entrance markings (see page 116) when upright signs indicate a prohibition of stopping.

Laws RTRO Art 4(5) & R(RW)O

Parking

239 Use off-street parking areas, or bays marked out with white lines on the road as parking places, wherever possible. If you have to stop on the road side

- do not park facing against the traffic flow
- stop as close as you can to the side

Rule 239 Check before opening your door

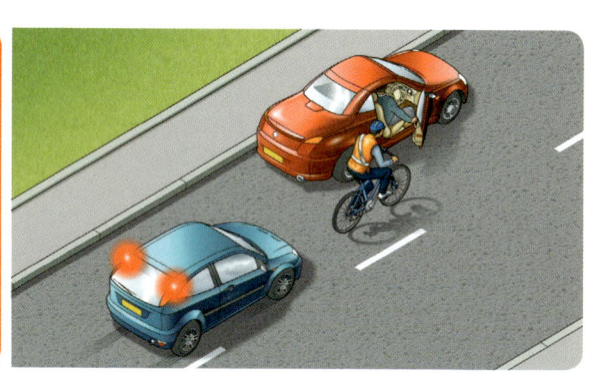

- do not stop too close to a vehicle displaying a Blue Badge, remember, the occupant may need more room to get in or out
- you **MUST** switch off the engine, headlights and fog lights
- you **MUST** apply the handbrake before leaving the vehicle

Waiting and parking

- you **MUST** ensure you do not hit anyone when you open your door. Check for cyclists or other traffic
- it is safer for your passengers (especially children) to get out of the vehicle on the side next to the kerb
- lock your vehicle.

Laws CUR regs 113, 121 & 123, RVLR reg 30, RTO 1995 Art 58 & R(RW)O

240 You **MUST NOT** stop or park on

- the carriageway or the hard shoulder of a motorway except in an emergency (see Rule 270)
- a pedestrian crossing, including the area marked by the zigzag lines (see Rule 191)
- within 15 metres (50 feet) of any junction, except in a lay-by in specified circumstances or in a designated parking area (see page 107)
- a clearway (see page 107)
- taxi bays as indicated by upright signs and markings
- an urban clearway within its hours of operation, except to pick up or set down passengers
- a road marked with double white lines, even when a broken white line is on your side of the road, except to pick up or set down passengers or to load or unload where this is not prohibited
- a bus stop marked on the carriageway or bus stop laybys unless otherwise indicated by signs
- a bus, tram or cycle lane during its period of operation
- a cycle track.

Laws RTO 1995 Art 32, RTRO Art 4(5), TSR Art 25, CUR reg 119 & R(RW)O

241 You **MUST NOT** park in parking spaces reserved for specific users, such as Blue Badge holders, residents or motorcycles, unless entitled to do so.

Laws RTRO Arts 14(1) & 19(1), & CSDPA sect 14B

242 You **MUST NOT** leave your vehicle or trailer in a dangerous position or where it causes any unnecessary obstruction of the road.

Laws RTO 1995 Art 32, RO Art 88 & CUR reg 119

243 **DO NOT** stop or park

- near a school entrance
- anywhere you would prevent access for Emergency Services
- at or near a bus stop or taxi rank
- on the approach to a level crossing/ tramway crossing
- near the brow of a hill or hump bridge
- opposite a traffic island or (if this would cause an obstruction) another parked vehicle
- where you would force other traffic to enter a tram lane
- where the kerb has been lowered to help wheelchair users and powered mobility vehicles
- in front of an entrance to a property
- on a bend
- where you would obstruct cyclists' use of cycle facilities

except when forced to do so by stationary traffic.

244 **DO NOT** park partially or wholly on the footway or footpath unless signs permit it. Parking on the footway or footpath can obstruct and seriously inconvenience pedestrians, people in wheelchairs or with visual impairments and people with prams or pushchairs.

245 **Controlled Parking Zones**. The zone entry signs indicate the times when the waiting restrictions within the zone are in force. Parking may be allowed in some places at other times. Otherwise parking will be within separately signed and marked bays.

Waiting and parking

246 **Goods vehicles.** Vehicles with a maximum laden weight of over 7.5 tonnes (including any trailer) **MUST NOT** be parked on a verge, footway or footpath or any land situated between carriageways, without police permission. The only exception is when parking is essential for loading and unloading, in which case the vehicle **MUST NOT** be left unattended.

Law RTO 1995 Art 30(1)

247 **Loading and unloading.** Do not load or unload where there are yellow markings on the kerb and upright signs advise that restrictions are in place (see pages 115–116). This may be permitted where parking is otherwise restricted.

Law RTRO Art 4(5)

Parking at night

248 You **MUST NOT** park on a road at night facing against the direction of the traffic flow unless in a recognised parking space.

Laws CUR reg 117 & RVLR reg 27

249 All vehicles **MUST** display parking lights when parked on a road or a lay-by on a road with a speed limit greater than 30 mph (48 km/h).

Law RVLR reg 27

250 Cars, goods vehicles not exceeding 2500 kg laden weight, invalid carriages, motorcycles and pedal cycles may be parked without lights on a road (or lay-by) with a speed limit of 30 mph (48 km/h) or less if they are

- at least 15 metres (50 feet) away from any junction, close to the kerb and facing in the direction of the traffic flow
- in a recognised parking place or lay-by.

Other vehicles and trailers, and all vehicles with projecting loads, **MUST NOT** be left on a road at night without lights.

Laws RVLR reg 27, R(RW)O & CUR reg 94(9)

Parking in fog

251 It is especially dangerous to park on the road in fog. If it is unavoidable, leave your parking lights or sidelights on.

Parking on hills

252 If you park on a hill you should

- park close to the kerb and apply the handbrake firmly
- select a forward gear and turn your steering wheel away from the kerb when facing uphill
- select reverse gear and turn your steering wheel towards the kerb when facing downhill
- use 'park' if your car has an automatic gearbox.

Rule 252 Turn your wheels away from the kerb when parking facing uphill. Turn them towards the kerb when parking facing downhill

Facing uphill

Facing downhill

Decriminalised Parking Enforcement (DPE)

DPE, already in place in Northern Ireland, is becoming increasingly common throughout the United Kingdom as more authorities take on this role. The Department for Infrastructure's TransportNI or the local traffic authorities in Great Britain assume responsibility for enforcing many parking contraventions in place of the police. Further details on DPE may be found at the following websites:

- www.nidirect.gov.uk/information-and-services/travel-transport-and-roads/parking-and-parking-enforcement
- www.trafficpenaltytribunal.gov.uk (outside London)
- www.londontribunals.gov.uk (inside London)

Motorways

Many other Rules apply to motorway driving, either wholly or in part: Rules 45, 57, 83–126, 130–134, 139, 144, 146–151, 160–161, 219, 221–222, 225, 226–237, 274–278, 280–287 and 288–290.

General

253 **Prohibited vehicles.** Motorways **MUST NOT** be used by pedestrians, holders of provisional motorcycle or car licences, riders of motorcycles under 50cc, cyclists, horse riders, certain slow-moving vehicles and those carrying oversized loads (except by special permission), agricultural vehicles, and powered wheelchairs/powered mobility scooters (see Rules 34–46 incl.).

Laws RO Art 16 & sch 1, & MTR reg 2

254 Traffic on motorways usually travels faster than on other roads, so you have less time to react. It is especially important to use your mirrors earlier and look much further ahead than you would on other roads.

Motorway signals

255 Motorway signals (see page 102) are used to warn you of a danger ahead. For example, there may be an incident, fog, a spillage, or road workers on the carriageway which you may not immediately be able to see.

256 Signals situated on the central reservation apply to all lanes. On very busy stretches, signals may be overhead with a separate signal for each lane.

257 **Amber flashing lights.** These warn of a hazard ahead. The signal may show a temporary maximum speed limit, lanes that are closed or a message such as 'Fog'. Adjust your speed and look out for the danger until you pass a signal which is not flashing or one that gives the 'All clear' and you are sure it is safe to increase your speed.

258 **Red flashing lights**. If red lights on the overhead signals flash above your lane and a red 'X' is showing, you **MUST NOT** go beyond the signal in that lane. If red lights flash on a signal in the central reservation or at the side of the road, you **MUST NOT** go beyond the signal in any lane.

Laws RTO 1995 Art 50 & TSR regs 8 & 33(3)

Driving on the motorway

259 **Joining the motorway.** When you join the motorway you will normally approach it from a road on the left (a slip-road) or from an adjoining motorway. You should

- give priority to traffic already on the motorway
- check the traffic on the motorway and match your speed to fit safely into the traffic flow in the left-hand lane
- not cross solid white lines that separate lanes or use the hard shoulder
- stay on the slip-road if it continues as an extra lane on the motorway
- remain in the left-hand lane long enough to adjust to the speed of traffic before considering overtaking.

On the motorway

260 When you can see well ahead and the road conditions are good, you should

- drive at a steady cruising speed which you and your vehicle can handle safely and is within the speed limit (see table on page 40)
- keep a safe distance from the vehicle in front and increase the gap on wet or icy roads, or in fog (see Rules 126 and 235).

Motorways

261 You **MUST NOT** exceed 70 mph (112 km/h), or the maximum speed limit permitted for your vehicle (see page 40). If a lower speed limit is in force, either permanently or temporarily, at road works for example, you **MUST NOT** exceed the lower limit. On some motorways, mandatory motorway signals (which display the speed within a red ring) are used to vary the speed limit to improve traffic flow. You **MUST NOT** exceed this speed limit.

Laws RO Art 20, RTRO Art 39 & MV(SL)R

262 The monotony of driving on a motorway can make you feel sleepy. To minimise the risk, follow the advice in Rule 91.

263 You **MUST NOT** reverse, cross the central reservation, or drive against the traffic flow. If you have missed your exit, or have taken the wrong route, carry on to the next exit.

Law MTR regs 4, 7 & 10

Lane discipline

264 You should always drive in the left-hand lane when the road ahead is clear. If you are overtaking a number of slower moving vehicles, you should return to the left-hand lane as soon as you are safely past. Slow-moving or speed-restricted vehicles should always remain in the left-hand lane of the carriageway unless overtaking. You **MUST NOT** drive on the hard shoulder except in an emergency or if directed to do so by the police or signs.

Law MTR regs 3 & 8

265 The right-hand lane of a motorway with three or more lanes should not be used if you are driving

- any vehicle drawing a trailer
- a goods vehicle with a maximum laden weight exceeding 3.5 tonnes but not exceeding 7.5 tonnes, which is required to be fitted with a speed limiter
- a goods vehicle with a maximum laden weight exceeding 7.5 tonnes

- a passenger vehicle with a maximum laden weight exceeding 7.5 tonnes constructed or adapted to carry more than eight seated passengers in addition to the driver
- a passenger vehicle with a maximum laden weight not exceeding 7.5 tonnes which is constructed or adapted to carry more than eight seated passengers in addition to the driver, which is required to be fitted with a speed limiter.

266 **Approaching a junction**. Look well ahead for signals or signs. Direction signs may be placed over the road. If you need to change lanes, do so in good time. At some junctions a lane may lead directly off the motorway. Only get in that lane if you wish to go in the direction indicated on the overhead signs.

Overtaking

267 Do not overtake unless you are sure it is safe and legal to do so. Overtake only on the right. You should

- check your mirrors
- take time to judge the speeds correctly
- make sure the lane you will be joining is sufficiently clear ahead and behind
- take a quick sideways glance into the blind spot area to verify the position of a vehicle that may have disappeared from your view in the mirror
- remember that traffic may be coming up behind you very quickly. Check all mirrors carefully. Look out for motorcyclists. When it is safe to do so, signal in plenty of time, then move out
- ensure you do not cut in on the vehicle you have overtaken
- be especially careful at night and in poor visibility when it is harder to judge speed and distance.

Motorways

268 Do not overtake on the left or move to a lane on your left to overtake. In congested conditions, where adjacent lanes of traffic are moving at similar speeds, traffic in left-hand lanes may sometimes be moving faster than traffic to the right. In these conditions you may keep up with the traffic in your lane even if this means passing traffic in the lane to your right. Do not weave in and out of lanes to overtake.

269 **Hard shoulder**. You **MUST NOT** use the hard shoulder for overtaking. In areas where an Active Traffic Management (ATM) scheme is in force, the hard shoulder may be used as a running lane. You will know when you can use this because a speed limit sign will be shown above all open lanes, including the hard shoulder. A red cross or blank sign above the hard shoulder means that you **MUST NOT** drive on the hard shoulder except in an emergency or breakdown. Emergency refuge areas have also been built into these areas for use in cases of emergency or breakdown.

Hard shoulder bus lanes. On some stretches of motorway, hard shoulders are used as bus lanes during specified times of the day. The operation of these bus lanes is controlled using variable message signing. In the event of an emergency or incident the bus lane reverts to being a hard shoulder. You **MUST NOT** use the bus lane for any purpose other than an emergency or breakdown.

Law MTR regs 3 & 8

Rule 269 Overhead gantry showing red cross over hard shoulder

Stopping

270 You **MUST NOT** stop on the carriageway, hard shoulder, slip road, central reservation or verge except in an emergency, or when told to do so by the police, an emergency sign or by flashing red light signals. Do not stop on the hard shoulder to either make or receive mobile phone calls.

Law MTR regs 5, 8 & 10

271 You **MUST NOT** pick up or set down anyone, or walk on a motorway, except in an emergency.

Laws RO Art 20 & MTR reg 13

Leaving the motorway

272 Unless signs indicate that a lane leads directly off the motorway, you will normally leave the motorway by a slip-road on your left. You should

- watch out for the signs letting you know you are getting near your exit
- move into the left-hand lane well before reaching your exit
- signal left in good time and reduce your speed on the slip road as necessary.

273 On leaving the motorway or using a link road between motorways, your speed may be higher than you realise – 50 mph (80 km/h) may feel like 30 mph (48 km/h). Check your speedometer and adjust your speed accordingly. Some slip roads and link roads have sharp bends, so you will need to slow down.

What signals would you expect from this person?

Turn to rule 105 and see page 105

Breakdowns and incidents

Breakdowns

274 If your vehicle breaks down, think first of all other road users and

- get your vehicle off the road if possible
- warn other traffic by using your hazard warning lights if your vehicle is causing an obstruction
- help other road users see you by wearing light coloured fluorescent clothing in daylight and reflective clothing at night or in poor visibility
- put a warning triangle on the road at least 45 metres (147 feet) behind your broken-down vehicle on the same side of the road, or use other permitted warning devices if you have them. Always take great care when placing or retrieving them, but never use them on motorways
- keep your side lights on if it is dark or visibility is poor
- do not stand (or let anybody else stand) between your vehicle and oncoming traffic
- at night or in poor visibility do not stand where you will prevent other road users seeing your lights.

Additional rules for the motorway

275 If your vehicle develops a problem, leave the motorway at the next exit or pull into a service area. If you cannot do so, you should

- pull onto the hard shoulder and stop as far to the left as possible, with your wheels turned to the left
- try to stop near an emergency telephone (situated at approximately one mile intervals along the hard shoulder)
- leave the vehicle by the left-hand door and ensure your passengers do the same. You **MUST** leave any animals in the vehicle or, in an emergency, keep them under proper control on the verge. Never attempt to place a warning triangle on a motorway

- not put yourself in danger by attempting even simple repairs
- ensure that passengers keep away from the carriageway and hard shoulder, and that children are kept under control

Rule 275 Keep well back from the hard shoulder

- walk to an emergency telephone on your side of the carriageway (follow the arrows on the posts at the back of the hard shoulder) – the telephone is free of charge and connects directly to the police. Use these in preference to a mobile phone (see Rule 283). Always face the traffic when you speak on the phone
- give full details to the police; also inform them if you are a vulnerable motorist such as disabled, older or travelling alone
- return and wait near your vehicle (well away from the carriageway and hard shoulder)
- if you feel at risk from another person, return to your vehicle by a left-hand door and lock all doors. Leave your vehicle again as soon as you feel this danger has passed.

Law MTR regs 12 & 13

276 Before you rejoin the carriageway after a breakdown, build up speed on the hard shoulder and watch for a safe gap in the traffic. Be aware that other vehicles may be stationary on the hard shoulder.

277 If you cannot get your vehicle onto the hard shoulder

- do not attempt to place any warning device on the carriageway
- switch on hazard warning lights
- leave your vehicle only when you can safely get clear of the carriageway.

278 **Disabled drivers**. If you have a disability which prevents you from following the above advice you should

- stay in your vehicle
- switch on hazard warning lights
- display a 'Help' pennant or, if you have a car or mobile telephone, contact the emergency services and be prepared to advise them of your location.

Obstructions

279 If anything falls from your vehicle (or any other vehicle) on to the road, stop and retrieve it only if it is safe to do so.

280 **Motorways**. On a motorway do not try to remove the obstruction yourself. Stop at the next emergency telephone and call the police.

Incidents

281 **Warning signs or flashing lights**. If you see or hear emergency or incident support vehicles in the distance be aware there may be an incident ahead (see Rule 219). Police officers and TransportNI officials may be required to work in the carriageway, for example dealing with debris, collisions or conducting rolling road blocks. Police officers will use rear-facing flashing red and blue lights in these situations. Watch out for such signals, slow down and be prepared to stop. You **MUST** follow any directions given by police officers as to whether you can safely pass the incident or blockage.

Laws RTO 1995 Art 49 & RTO 1981 Art 180

282 When passing the scene of an incident or crash do not be distracted or slow down unnecessarily (for example if an incident is on the other side of a dual carriageway). This may cause a collision or traffic congestion, but see Rule 283.

283 If you are involved in a collision or stop to give assistance

- use your hazard warning lights to warn other traffic
- ask drivers to switch off their engines and stop smoking
- arrange for the emergency services to be called immediately with full details of the incident location and any casualties (on a motorway, use the emergency telephone which allows easy location by the emergency services. If you use a mobile phone, first make sure you have identified your location from the marker posts on the side of the hard shoulder)
- move uninjured people away from the vehicles to safety; on a motorway this should, if possible, be well away from the traffic, the hard shoulder and the central reservation
- do not move injured people from their vehicles unless they are in immediate danger from fire or explosion
- do not remove a motorcyclist's helmet unless it is essential to do so
- be prepared to give first aid as shown on pages 131–133
- stay at the scene until emergency services arrive.

If you are involved in any other medical emergency on the motorway you should contact the emergency services in the same way.

Incidents involving dangerous goods

284 Vehicles carrying dangerous goods in packages will be marked with plain orange reflective plates. Road tankers and vehicles carrying tank containers of dangerous goods will have hazard warning plates (see page 117).

285 If an incident involves a vehicle containing dangerous goods, follow the advice in Rule 283 and, in particular

- switch off engines and **DO NOT SMOKE**
- keep well away from the vehicle and do not be tempted to try to rescue casualties, as you yourself could become one
- call the emergency services and give as much information as possible about the labels and markings on the vehicle. Do not use a mobile phone close to a vehicle carrying inflammable loads.

Documentation

286 If you are involved in a collision which causes damage or injury to any other person, vehicle, animal or property, you **MUST**

- stop
- give your own and the vehicle owner's name and address, and the registration number of the vehicle, to anyone having reasonable grounds for requiring them
- if you do not give your name and address at the time of the collision, report the collision to the police immediately.

Law RTO 1981 Arts 175 & 176

287 If another person is injured and you do not produce your insurance certificate at the time of the collision to a police officer, or to anyone having reasonable grounds for requesting it, you **MUST**

- report the collision to the police immediately
- produce your insurance certificate for the police as soon as reasonably practicable.

Law RTO 1981 Art 175

Road works

288 When the 'Road Works Ahead' sign is displayed, you will need to be more watchful and look for additional signs providing more specific instructions. Observe all signs – they are there for your safety and the safety of road workers.

- You **MUST NOT** exceed any temporary maximum speed limit.
- Use your mirrors and get into the correct lane for your vehicle in good time and as signs direct.
- Do not switch lanes to overtake queuing traffic.
- Take extra care near cyclists and motorcyclists as they are vulnerable to skidding on grit, mud and other debris at road works.
- Where lanes are restricted due to road works, merge in turn (see Rule 134).
- Do not drive through an area marked off by traffic cones.
- Watch out for traffic entering or leaving the works area, but do not be distracted by what is going on there. Concentrate on the road ahead, not the road works.
- Bear in mind that the road ahead may be obstructed by the works or by slow moving or stationary traffic.
- Keep a safe distance – there could be queues in front.

Law RTRO Art 43

Additional rules for high-speed roads

289 Take special care on motorways and other high-speed dual carriageways.

- One or more lanes may be closed to traffic and a lower speed limit may apply.
- Works vehicles that are slow moving or stationary with a large 'Keep Left' or 'Keep Right' sign on the back are sometimes used to close lanes for repairs, and a flashing light arrow may also be used to make the

works vehicle more conspicuous from a distance and give earlier warning to drivers that they need to move over to the next lane.

- Check mirrors, slow down and change lanes if necessary.
- Keep a safe distance from the vehicle in front (see Rule 126).

290 Contraflow systems mean that you may be travelling in a narrower lane than normal and with no permanent barrier between you and oncoming traffic. The hard shoulder may be used for traffic, but be aware that there may be broken-down vehicles ahead of you. Keep a good distance from the vehicle ahead and observe any temporary speed limits.

Level crossings

291 A level crossing is where a road crosses a railway or tramway line. Approach and cross it with care. Never drive onto a crossing until the road is clear on the other side and do not get too close to the car in front. Never stop or park on, or near, a crossing.

292 **Overhead electric lines.** It is dangerous to touch overhead electric lines. You **MUST** obey the safe height warning road signs and you should not continue forward onto the railway if your vehicle touches any height barrier or bells. The clearance available is usually 5 metres (16 feet 6 inches) but may be lower.

Laws RTO 1995 Art 50(1) & TSR reg 15(2)

293 **Controlled crossings.** Most crossings have traffic light signals with a steady amber light, twin flashing red stop lights (see page 102 and 109) and an audible alarm for pedestrians. They may have full, half or no barriers.

- You **MUST** always obey the flashing red stop lights.
- You **MUST** stop behind the white line across the road.

Rule 293
Stop when the traffic lights show

- Keep going if you have already crossed the white line when the amber light comes on.

- Do not reverse onto or over a controlled crossing.

- You **MUST** wait if a train goes by and the red lights continue to flash. This means another train will be passing soon.

- Only cross when the lights go off, and the barriers open.

- Never zigzag around half-barriers; they lower automatically because a train is approaching.

- At crossings where there are no barriers, a train is approaching when the lights show.

Laws RTO 1995 Art 50 & TSR regs 8 & 33

294 **Railway telephones.** If you are driving a large or slow-moving vehicle, a long, low vehicle with a risk of grounding, or herding animals, a train could arrive before you are clear of the crossing. You **MUST** obey any sign instructing you to use the railway telephone to obtain permission to cross. You **MUST** also telephone when clear of the crossing if requested to do so.

Laws RTO 1995 Art 50 & TSR regs 8 & 14

295 **Crossings without traffic lights.** Vehicles should stop and wait at the barrier or gate when it begins to close and not cross until the barrier or gate opens.

Level crossings

296 **User-operated gates or barriers**. Some crossings have 'Stop' signs and small red and green lights. You **MUST NOT** cross when the red light is showing; only cross if the green light is on. If crossing with a vehicle you should

- open the gates or barriers on both sides of the crossing
- check that the green light is still on and cross quickly
- close the gates or barriers when you are clear of the crossing.

Laws RTO 1995 Art 50 & TSR reg 8

297 If there are no lights, follow the procedure in Rule 296. Stop, look both ways and listen before you cross. If there is a railway telephone, always use it to contact the signal operator to make sure it is safe to cross. Inform the signal operator again when you are clear of the crossing.

298 **Open crossings.** These have no gates, barriers, attendant or traffic lights but will have a 'Give Way' sign. You should look both ways, listen and make sure there is no train coming before you cross.

299 **Incidents and breakdowns**. If your vehicle breaks down, or if you have a collision on a crossing you should

- get everyone out of the vehicle and clear of the crossing immediately
- use a railway telephone if available to tell the signal operator. Follow the instructions you are given
- move the vehicle clear of the crossing if there is time before a train arrives. If the alarm sounds, or the amber light comes on, leave the vehicle and get clear of the crossing immediately.

Tramways

Currently applies to Great Britain only. Legislative references relate to Great Britain legislation.

300 You **MUST NOT** enter a road, lane or other route reserved for trams. Take extra care where trams run along the road. You should avoid driving directly on top of the rails and should take care where trams leave the main carriageway to enter the reserved route, to ensure you do not follow them. The width taken up by trams is often shown by tram lanes marked by white lines, yellow dots, or by a different type of road surface. Diamond-shaped signs and white light signals give instructions to tram drivers only.

Law RTRA sects 5 & 8

301 Take extra care where the track crosses from one side of the road to the other and where the road narrows and the tracks come close to the kerb. Tram drivers usually have their own traffic signals and may be permitted to move when you are not. Always give way to trams. Do not try to race or overtake them, or pass them on the inside, unless they are at tram stops or stopped by tram signals and there is a designated tram lane for you to pass.

302 You **MUST NOT** park your vehicle where it would get in the way of trams or where it would force other drivers to do so. Do not stop on any part of a tram track except in a designated bay where this has been provided alongside and clear of the track. When doing so, ensure that all parts of your vehicle are outside the delineated tram path. Remember that a train cannot steer round an obstruction.

Law RTRA sects 5 & 8

303 **Tram stops.** Where the tram stops at a platform, either in the middle or at the side of the road, you **MUST** follow the route shown by the road signs and markings. At stops without platforms you **MUST NOT** drive between a tram and the left-hand kerb when a tram has stopped to pick up passengers. If there is no alternative route signed do not overtake the tram – wait until it moves off.

Law RTRA sects 5 & 8

Tramways

304 Look out for pedestrians, especially children, running to catch a tram approaching a stop.

305 Always give priority to trams, especially when they signal to pull away from stops, unless it would be unsafe to do so. Remember that they may be carrying large numbers of standing passengers who could be injured if the tram had to make an emergency stop. Look out for people getting off a bus or tram and crossing the road.

306 All road users, but particularly cyclists and motorcyclists, should take extra care when driving or riding close to or crossing the tracks, especially if the rails are wet. You should take particular care when crossing the rails at shallow angles, on bends and at junctions. It is safest to cross the track directly at right angles. Other road users should be aware that cyclists and motorcyclists need more space to cross the tracks safely.

307 **Overhead electric lines**. Tramway overhead wires are normally 5.8 metres above any carriageway, but can be lower. You should ensure that you have sufficient clearance between the wire and your vehicle (including any load you are carrying) before driving under an overhead wire. Drivers of vehicles with extending cranes, boom, tipping apparatus or other types of variable height equipment should ensure that the equipment is fully lowered. Where overhead wires are set lower than 5.8 metres, these will be indicated by height clearance markings – similar to 'low bridge' signs. The height clearances on these plates should be carefully noted and observed. If you are in any doubt as to whether you vehicle will pass safely under the wires you should always contact the local police or the tramway operator. Never take a chance as this can be extremely hazardous.

Light signals controlling traffic

Traffic light signals

RED means 'Stop'. Wait behind the stop line on the carriageway

RED AND AMBER also means 'Stop'. Do not pass through or start until GREEN shows

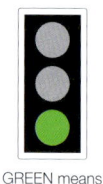

GREEN means you may go on if the way is clear. Take special care if you intend to turn left or right and give way to pedestrians who are crossing

AMBER means 'Stop' at the stop line. You may go on only if the AMBER appears after you have crossed the stop line or are so close to it that to pull up might cause a collision

A GREEN ARROW may be provided in addition to the full green signal if movement in a certain direction is allowed before or after the full green phase. If the way is clear you may go but only in the direction shown by the arrow. You may do this whatever other lights may be showing. White light signals may be provided for trams

Flashing red lights

Alternately flashing red lights mean YOU MUST STOP

At level crossings, lifting bridges, airfields, fire stations, etc.

Motorway signals

You **MUST NOT** proceed further in this lane

Change lane

Reduced visibility ahead

Lane ahead closed

Temporary maximum speed advised and information message

Leave motorway at next exit

Temporary maximum speed advised

End of restriction

Lane control signals

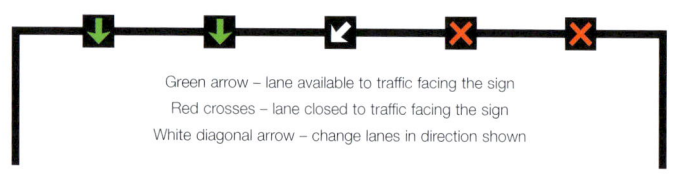

Green arrow – lane available to traffic facing the sign
Red crosses – lane closed to traffic facing the sign
White diagonal arrow – change lanes in direction shown

Signals to other road users

Direction indicator signals

I intend to move out to the right or turn right

I intend to move in to the left or turn left or stop on the left

Brake light signals

I am applying the brakes

Reversing light signals

I intend to reverse

These signals should not be used except for the purposes described.

Arm signals

For use when direction indicator signals are not used, or when necessary to reinforce direction indicator signals and stop lights. *Also for use by pedal cyclists and those in charge of horses*.

I intend to move in to the left or turn left

I intend to move out to the right or turn right

I intend to slow down or stop

Signals by authorised persons

Police officers

Stop

Traffic approaching from the front

Traffic approaching from both front and behind

Traffic approaching from behind

To beckon traffic on

From the side

From the front

From behind

Arm signals to persons controlling traffic

I want to go straight on

I want to turn left; use either hand

I want to turn right

Driver and Vehicle Agency

Driver and Vehicle Agency Enforcement Officer

These officers have powers to stop/direct vehicles and will be using hand signals and light signals similar to those used by police. You **MUST** obey any signals given (see Rule 107).

School crossing patrols

Not ready to cross children

Barrier to stop children crossing

Ready to cross children, vehicles must be prepared to stop

All vehicles must stop

105

Traffic signs

Signs giving orders

Signs with red circles are mostly prohibitive. Plates below signs qualify their message.

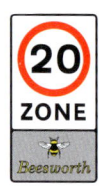

Entry to 20 mph zone	End of 20 mph zone	Maximum speed	 National speed limit applies	School crossing patrol
 Stop and give way	Give way to traffic on major road	Manually operated temporary STOP and GO signs		 No entry for vehicular traffic
No vehicles except bicycles being pushed	 No cycling	 No motor vehicles	 No buses (over 8 passenger seats)	 No overtaking
 No towed caravans	 No vehicles carrying explosives	No vehicle or combination of vehicles over length shown	No vehicles over height shown	No vehicles over width shown
Give priority to vehicles from opposite direction	 No right turn	 No left turn	 No U-turns	No goods vehicles over maximum gross weight shown (in tonnes) except for loading and unloading

Note: Although *The Highway Code* shows many of the signs commonly in use, a comprehensive explanation of our signing system is given in the booklet *Know Your Traffic Signs*, which is on sale at booksellers. The booklet also illustrates and explains the vast majority of signs the road user is likely to encounter. The signs illustrated in *The Highway Code* are not all drawn to the same scale.

WEAK BRIDGE
18t m g w

No vehicles over maximum gross weight shown (in tonnes)

Permit holders only

Parking restricted to permit holders

RED ROUTE — No stopping at any time except buses

No stopping during period indicated except for buses

URBAN CLEARWAY Monday to Friday
am 8.00 - 9.30   pm 4.30 - 6.30

No stopping during times shown except for as long as necessary to set down or pick up passengers

No waiting

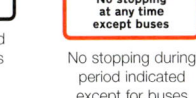

No stopping (Clearway)

Signs with blue circles but no red border mostly give positive instruction.

Ahead only

Turn left ahead (right if symbol reversed)

Turn left (right if symbol reversed)

Keep left (right if symbol reversed)

Vehicles may pass either side to reach same destination

Mini-roundabout (roundabout circulation - give way to vehicles from the immediate right)

Route to be used by pedal cycles only

Segregated pedal cycle and pedestrian route

Minimum speed

End of minimum speed

Buses and cycles only

Trams only

TRAMWAY LOOK BOTH WAYS

Pedestrian crossing point over tramway

One-way traffic (note: compare circular 'Ahead only' sign)

With-flow bus and cycle lane

Contra-flow bus lane

With-flow pedal cycle lane

107

Warning signs

Mostly triangular

- Distance to 'STOP' line ahead
- Dual carriageway ends
- Road narrows on right (left if symbol reversed)
- Road narrows on both sides
- Distance to 'Give Way' line ahead

- Crossroads
- Junction on bend ahead
- T-junction with priority over vehicles from the right
- Staggered junction
- Traffic merging from left ahead

The priority through route is indicated by the broader line.

- Double bend first to left (symbol may be reversed)
- Bend to right (or left if symbol reversed)
- Roundabout
- Uneven road
- Plate below some signs

- Two-way traffic crosses one-way road
- Two-way traffic straight ahead
- Opening or swing bridge ahead
- Low-flying aircraft or sudden aircraft noise
- Falling or fallen rocks

- Traffic signals not in use
- Traffic signals
- Slippery road
- Steep hill downwards
- Steep hill upwards

Gradients may be shown as a ratio i.e. 20% = 1:5

- Tunnel ahead
- Trams crossing ahead
- Level crossing with barrier or gate ahead
- Level crossing without barrier or gate ahead
- Level crossing without barrier

Warning signs - continued

School crossing patrol ahead (some signs have amber lights which flash when crossings are in use)

Frail (or blind or disabled if shown) pedestrians likely to cross road ahead

Pedestrians in road ahead

Zebra crossing

Overhead electric cable; plate indicates maximum height of vehicles which can pass safely

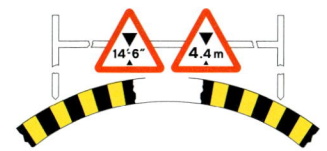

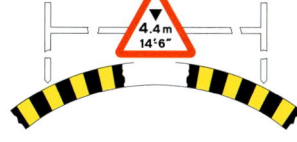

Available width of headroom indicated (alternatives)

Sharp deviation of route to left (or right if chevrons reversed)

Light signals ahead at level crossing, airfield or bridge

Miniature warning lights at level crossing

Cattle

Wild animals

Wild horses or ponies

Accompanied horses or ponies

Cycle route ahead

Risk of ice

Traffic queues likely ahead

Distance over which road humps extend

Other danger; plate indicates nature of danger

Soft verges

Side winds

Hump bridge

Worded warning sign

Quayside or river bank

Risk of grounding

Direction signs

Mostly rectangular

Signs on motorways - blue backgrounds

Craigavon 11 M1

At a junction leading directly into a motorway (junction number may be shown on a black background)

Broughshane A42 11 1½m

On approaches to junctions (junction number on black background)

M1 The WEST Craigavon 21 Newry 31

Route confirmatory sign after junction

A2 Queen's Island Belfast(E), Newcastle 1 ⅓m

City Airport ✈ Bangor, Newtownards M3

Downward pointing arrows mean 'Get in lane'
The left-hand lane leads to a different destination from the other lanes.

↖ A12 (M1) Lisburn, Craigavon

2 ½m The NORTH, Larne, Coleraine, Londonderry M2 ↑

The panel with the inclined arrow indicates the destinations which can be reached by leaving the motorway at the next junction

Signs on primary routes - green backgrounds

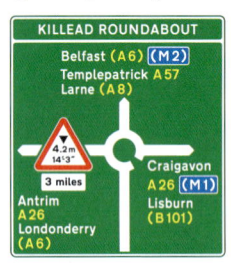

KILLEAD ROUNDABOUT
Belfast (A6) (M2)
Templepatrick A57
Larne (A8)
4.2m 14'3" 3 miles
Craigavon A26 (M1)
Antrim A26
Lisburn (B101)
Londonderry (A6)

On approaches to junctions

BALLINDERRY CROSSROADS
↑ Moira A26
Craigavon (M1)
Lower B'derry B104 →
Lisburn B104
← Irish Linen Centre 🏛

On approaches to junctions

Antrim Ballymena A26 4.2m 14'3" 3 miles →

At the junction

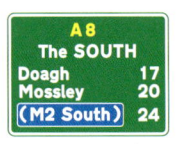

A8 The SOUTH
Doagh 17
Mossley 20
(M2 South) 24

Route confirmatory sign after junction

Strabane A5 ↗

On approach to a junction

Blue panels indicate that the motorway starts at the junction ahead.
Motorways shown in brackets can also be reached along the route indicated.
White panels indicate local or non-primary routes leading from the junction ahead.
Brown panels show the route to tourist attractions.
The name of the junction may be shown at the top of the sign.
The aircraft symbol indicates the route to an airport.
A symbol may be included to warn of a hazard or restriction along that route.

Green background signs - continued

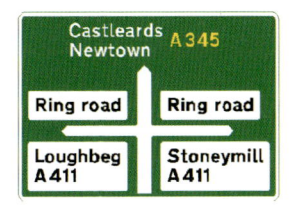

On approaches to junctions

Primary route forming part of a ring road

Signs on non-primary and local routes - black borders

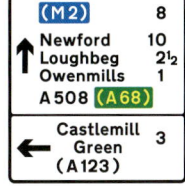

On approaches to junctions

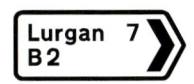

At the junction

Direction to toilets with access for the disabled

Green panels indicate that the primary route starts at the junction ahead.
Route numbers on a blue background show the direction to a motorway.
Route numbers on a green background show the direction to a primary route.

Other direction signs

Picnic site

National Trust Property

Direction to a car park

Tourist attraction

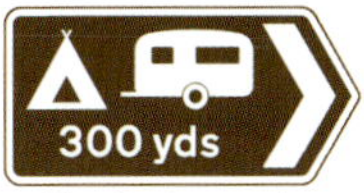

Direction to camping and caravan site

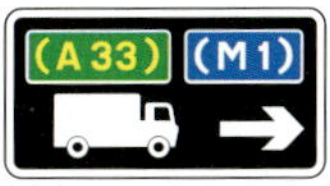

Advisory route for lorries

Route for pedal cycles forming part of a network

Recommended route for pedal cycles to place shown

Route for pedestrians

Symbols showing emergency diversion route for motorway and other main road traffic

Diversion route

Information signs

All rectangular

Entrance to controlled parking zone — Controlled ZONE, Mon-Fri 8.30 am - 6.30 pm, Saturday 8.30 am - 1.30 pm

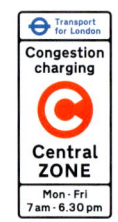

Entrance to congestion charging zone — Transport for London, Congestion charging, Central ZONE, Mon-Fri 7am - 6.30pm

End of controlled parking zone — Zone ENDS

Advance warning of restriction or prohibition ahead — Low bridge 2 miles ahead, 4.4 m 14'6"

Parking place for solo motorcycles

With-flow bus lane ahead which pedal cycles, motorcycles and taxis may also use — permitted taxi

Lane designated for use by high occupancy vehicles (HOV). See Rule 142 — 2+ Mon-Fri 7-9 am 4-6 pm

Vehicles permitted to use HOV lane ahead — 2+ lane, For vehicles with 2 or more persons & No HGVs over 7.5 t

End of motorway

Start of motorway and point from which motorway regulations apply — M 62

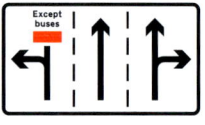

Appropriate traffic lanes at junction ahead — Except buses

Traffic on the main carriageway coming from right has priority over joining traffic

Additional traffic joining from left ahead. Traffic on main carriageway has priority over joining traffic from right-hand lane of slip road

Traffic in right-hand lane of slip road joining the main carriageway has priority over left hand lane

'Countdown' markers at exit from motorway (each bar represents 100 yards to the exit). Green-backed markers may be used on primary routes and white-backed markers with black bars on other routes. At approaches to concealed level crossings white-backed markers with red bars may be used. Although these will be erected at equal distances the bars do not represent 100 yard intervals.

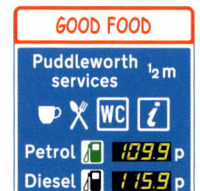

Motorway service area sign — GOOD FOOD, Puddleworth services ½ m, Petrol 109.9 p, Diesel 115.9 p

Information signs - continued

Traffic has priority over oncoming vehicles

Hospital ahead with Accident and Emergency facilities

Tourist information point

No through road for vehicles

Speed camera ahead and reminder of speed limit

Recommended route for pedal cycles

Home Zone Entry

Area in which cameras are used to enforce traffic regulations

Bus lane on road at junction ahead

Road works signs

Road works

Loose chippings

Temporary hazard at road works

Temporary lane closure (the number and position of arrows and red bars may be varied according to lanes open and closed)

Slow-moving or stationary works vehicle blocking a traffic lane. Pass in the direction shown by the arrow.

Mandatory speed limit ahead

Road works 1 mile ahead

End of road works and any temporary restrictions, including speed limits

Signs used on the back of slow-moving or stationary vehicles warning of a lane closed ahead by a works vehicle. There are no cones on the road.

Lane restrictions at road works ahead

One lane crossover at contraflow road works

Road markings

Across the carriageway

Stop line at signals or police control

Stop line at 'Stop' sign

Stop line for pedestrians at a level crossing

Give way to traffic on major road (can also be used at mini roundabouts)

Give way to traffic from the right at a roundabout

Give way to traffic from the right at a mini-roundabout

Along the carriageway

Edge line

Centre line, see Rule 127

Hazard warning line, see Rule 127

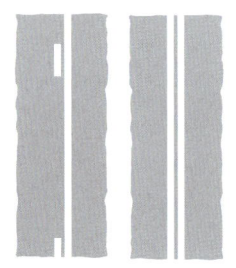

Double white lines, see Rules 128 and 129

See Rule 130

Lane line See Rule 131

Along the edge of the carriageway

Waiting restrictions

Waiting restrictions indicated by yellow lines apply to the carriageway, footway or footpath. You may stop to load or unload (unless there are also loading restrictions as described below) or while passengers board or alight. Double yellow lines mean no waiting at any time, unless there are signs that specifically indicate seasonal restrictions. The times at which the restrictions apply for other road markings are shown on nearby plates or on entry signs to controlled parking zones. If no days are shown on the signs, the restrictions are in force every day including Sundays and bank holidays. White bay markings and upright signs (see below) indicate where parking is allowed.

No waiting at any time

No waiting during times shown on sign

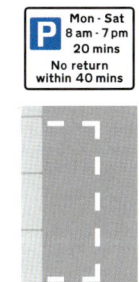

Waiting is limited to the duration specified during the days and times shown

Red Route stopping controls

Red lines are used on some roads instead of yellow lines. In London the double and single red lines used on Red Routes indicate that stopping to park, load/unload or to board and alight from a vehicle (except for a licensed taxi or if you hold a Blue Badge) is prohibited. The red lines apply to the carriageway, pavement and verge. The times that the red line prohibitions apply are shown on nearby signs, but the double red line ALWAYS means no stopping at any time. On Red Routes you may stop to park, load/unload in specially marked boxes and adjacent signs specify the times and purposes and duration allowed. A box MARKED IN RED indicates that it may only be available for the purpose specified for part of the day (eg between busy peak periods). A box MARKED IN WHITE means that it is available throughout the day.

RED AND SINGLE YELLOW LINES CAN ONLY GIVE A GUIDE TO THE RESTRICTIONS AND CONTROLS IN FORCE AND SIGNS, NEARBY OR AT A ZONE ENTRY, MUST BE CONSULTED.

No stopping at any time

No stopping during times shown on sign

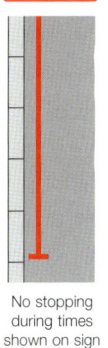

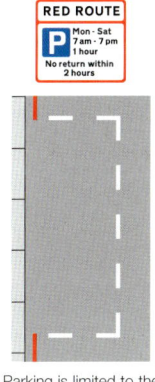

Parking is limited to the duration specified during the days and times shown

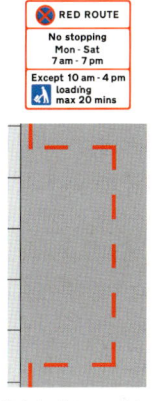

Only loading may take place at the times shown for up to a maximum duration of 20 mins

On the kerb or at the edge of the carriageway

Loading restrictions on roads other than Red Routes

Yellow marks on the kerb or at the edge of the carriageway indicate that loading or unloading is prohibited at the times shown on the nearby black and white plates. You may stop while passengers board or alight. If no days are indicated on the signs the restrictions are in force every day including Sundays and Bank Holidays.

ALWAYS CHECK THE TIMES SHOWN ON THE PLATES.

Lengths of road reserved for vehicles loading and unloading are indicated by a white 'bay' marking with the words 'Loading Only' and a sign with the white on blue 'trolley' symbol. This sign also shows whether loading and unloading is restricted to goods vehicles and the times at which the bay can be used. If no times or days are shown it may be used at any time. Vehicles may not park here if they are not loading or unloading.

No loading or unloading at any time

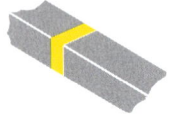

No loading or unloading at the times shown

Loading bay

Other road markings

Keep entrance clear of stationary vehicles, even if picking up or setting down children

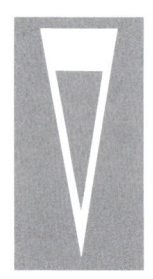

Warning of 'Give Way' just ahead

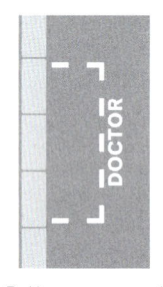

Parking space reserved for vehicles named

See Rules 240 & 243

See Rule 141

Box junction, see Rule 174

Do not block that part of the carriageway indicated

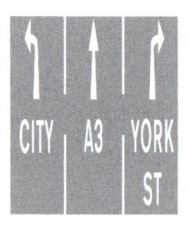

Indication of traffic lanes

Vehicle markings

Large goods vehicle rear markings

Motor vehicles over 7500 kilograms maximum gross weight and trailers over 3500 kilograms maximum gross weight

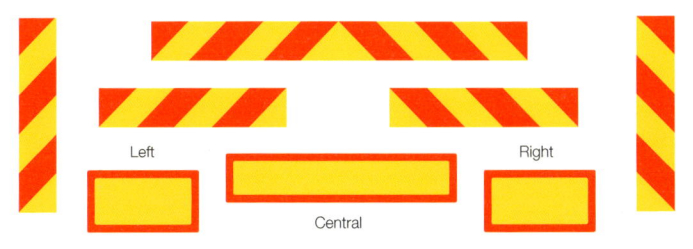

Left Right

Central

The vertical markings are also required to be fitted to builders' skips placed in the road, commercial vehicles or combinations longer than 13 metres
(optional on combinations between 11 and 13 metres)

Hazard warning plates

Certain tank vehicles carrying dangerous goods must display hazard information panels

The panel illustrated is for flammable liquid. Diamond symbols indicating other risks include:

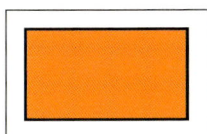

The above panel will be displayed by vehicles carrying certain dangerous goods in packages

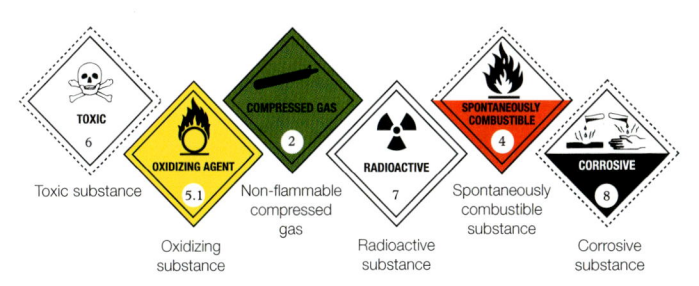

Toxic substance

Oxidizing substance

Non-flammable compressed gas

Radioactive substance

Spontaneously combustible substance

Corrosive substance

Projection markers

Side marker End marker

Both required when load or equipment (eg crane jib) overhangs front or rear by more than two metres

Other

School bus
(displayed in front or rear window of bus or coach)

Annexes

1. You and your bicycle

Make sure that you feel confident of your ability to ride safely on the road. Be sure that

- you choose the right size and type of cycle for comfort and safety
- lights and reflectors are kept clean and in good working order
- tyres are in good condition and inflated to the pressure shown on the tyre
- gears are working correctly
- the chain is properly adjusted and oiled
- the saddle and handlebars are adjusted to the correct height.

You **MUST**

- ensure your brakes are efficient
- ensure a working bell or horn is fitted
- at night, use lit front and rear lights and have a red rear reflector.

Laws RV(T)R reg 7 & RVLR reg 21

Cycle training can help both children and adults, especially those adults returning to cycling to develop the skills needed to cycle safely on today's roads.

All cyclists should consider the benefits of undertaking cycle training. For information, contact the Department for Infrastructure's Road Safety Promotion and Outreach Branch.

2. Motorcycle licence requirements

If you have a provisional motorcycle licence, you **MUST** satisfactorily complete a compulsory basic training (CBT) course.

You can then ride unaccompanied on the public road a motorcycle up to 125 cc with a power output not exceeding 11 kW, with L plates, for up to two years.

Law RTO 1981 Art 13

To ride a moped, learners **MUST**

- be 16 or over
- have a provisional moped licence
- complete CBT training.

Law RTO 1981 Arts 13 & 17

You can then ride unaccompanied on a public road a two-wheeled vehicle with a maximum design speed of 45 km/h (28 mph), with L plates, for up to two years.

You **MUST** first pass the theory test for motorcycles, the manoeuvres test and then the moped practical test to obtain your full moped licence.

Law MV(DL)R regs 27 & 32

If you passed your car driving test before 21 February 2011 you are qualified to ride a moped without L plates, although it is recommended that you complete CBT before riding on the road. If you passed your car driving test after this date you **MUST** complete CBT before riding a moped on the road.

Laws RTO 1981 Arts 13 & 17, & MV(DL)R regs 27 & 32

Licence categories for mopeds and motorcycles

Category AM (moped) – minimum age 16

- two-wheeled vehicle with a maximum design speed of 45 km/h (28 mph)
- three- or four-wheeled vehicle with a maximum design speed over 25 km/h (15.5 mph), up to 50 cc and with a power output not exceeding 4 kW.

Category A1 – minimum age 17

- motorcycles up to 125 cc, with a power output up to 11 kW
- tricycles with power not exceeding 15 kW.

Category A2 – minimum age 19

- motorcycles with a power output not exceeding 35 kW and with a power-to-weight ratio not exceeding 0.2 kW/kg.

Category A

- unrestricted motorcycles with a power output over 35 kW (minimum age 24 under direct access, or 21 under progressive access)
- tricycles with a power output over 15 kW (minimum age 21).

Progressive access is a process that allows a rider to take a higher-category practical test if they already have at least two years' experience on a lower-category motorcycle. If you have held a category A2 licence for a minimum of two years, you can take the category A practical test at age 21. There is no requirement to take another theory test.

If you want to learn to ride motorcycles larger than 125 cc and with a power output over 11 kW, you **MUST** meet the minimum age requirements, satisfactorily complete a CBT course and be accompanied by an approved instructor on another motorcycle in radio contact.

Laws MV(DL)R regs 6 & 12, & RTO 1981 Art 13

To obtain your full moped or motorcycle licence you **MUST** pass a motorcycle theory test, manoeuvres test and practical motorcycle test on a two-wheeled motorcycle.

Law MV(DL)R reg 27

You **MUST NOT** carry a pillion passenger or pull a trailer until you have passed your test. Also see Rule 253 covering vehicles prohibited from motorways.

Law MV(DL)R reg 12

3. Motor vehicle documentation, learner and restricted driver requirements

Documents
Driving licence. You **MUST** have a valid signed driving licence for the category of vehicle you are driving. You **MUST** inform the Driver and Vehicle Agency (DVA) if you change your name and address.

Law RTO 1981 Art 3

Holders of non-European Community licences who are now resident in the UK may only drive on that licence for a maximum of 12 months from the date they become resident in this country.

To ensure continuous driving entitlement

- a UK provisional licence should be obtained and a driving test(s) passed before the 12-month period elapses, or
- in the case of a driver who holds a licence from a country which has been designated in law for licence exchange purposes, the driver should exchange the licence for a UK one.

MOT. Cars and motorcycles **MUST** normally pass an MOT test (vehicle test) four years from the date of the first registration and every year after that. You **MUST NOT** drive a motor vehicle without an MOT certificate when it should have one. Exceptionally, you may drive to a pre-arranged test appointment or to a garage for repairs required for the test. Driving an unroadworthy motor vehicle may invalidate your insurance. From 30 September 2013, motor vehicles manufactured before 1960 will be exempted from an MOT requirement, although they can still be submitted for a test voluntarily. Owners are still legally required to ensure their vehicle is safe and roadworthy.

Law RTO 1995 Arts 61, 63, 65 & 69

Insurance. To use a motor vehicle on the road, you **MUST** have a valid insurance policy. This **MUST** at least cover you for injury or damage to a third party while using that motor vehicle. Before driving any motor vehicle, make sure that it has this cover for your use, or that your own insurance provides adequate cover. You **MUST NOT** drive a motor vehicle without insurance. Also, be aware that even if a road traffic collision is not your fault, you may still be held liable by insurance companies.

Law RTO 1981 Art 90

Uninsured drivers can now be automatically detected by roadside cameras.

The types of insurance cover are indicated as follows.

Third-party insurance – this is often the cheapest form of insurance, and is the minimum cover required by law. It covers anyone you might injure or whose property you might damage. It does not cover damage to your own motor vehicle or injury to yourself.

Third-party, Fire and Theft insurance – similar to third-party, but also covers you against your motor vehicle being stolen, or damaged by fire.

Comprehensive insurance – this is usually the most expensive but the best insurance. Apart from covering other persons and property against injury or damage, it also covers damage to your own motor vehicle, up to the market value of that vehicle, and personal injury to yourself.

Registration certificate. Registration certificates (also called harmonised registration certificates) are issued for all motor vehicles used on the road, describing them (make, model, etc.) and giving details of the registered keeper. You **MUST** notify the Driver and Vehicle Licensing Agency in Swansea as soon as possible when you buy or sell a motor vehicle, or if you change your name or address. The seller is responsible for advising DVLA there has been a change of registered keeper. The procedures are explained on the back of the registration certificates and at **www.gov.uk** ('Tell DVLA you've sold, transferred or bought a vehicle').

Law RV(R&L)R Part IV

Vehicle tax. Vehicle tax **MUST** be paid on all motor vehicles used or kept on public roads.

Law VERA sects 29 & 33

Statutory Off Road Notification (SORN). This is a notification to the Driver and Vehicle Licensing Agency in Swansea that a vehicle is not being used on the road. If you want to keep a vehicle untaxed and off the public road you **MUST** declare SORN – it is an offence not to do so. A SORN will remain in force until the vehicle is taxed, sold or scrapped. If your vehicle is unused or off the road, it **MUST** either have a SORN declaration or be taxed.

Law RV(R&L)R reg 26 sch 4

Production of documents. You **MUST** be able to produce your driving licence and counterpart, a valid insurance certificate and (if appropriate) a valid MOT certificate, when requested by a police officer. If you cannot do this you may be asked to take them to a police station within seven days.

Law RTO 1981 Arts 180 & 180A

Learner drivers

Learners driving a car **MUST** hold a valid provisional licence. They **MUST** be supervised by someone at least 21 years old who holds a full EC/EEA licence for that type of car (automatic or manual) and has held one for at least three years.

Laws MV(DL)R reg 12 & RTO 1981 Art 3

Vehicles. Any vehicle driven by a learner **MUST** display red L plates. Plates **MUST** conform to legal specifications and **MUST** be clearly visible to others from in front of the vehicle and from behind. Plates should be removed or covered when not being driven by a learner (except on driving school vehicles.)

The speed limit for vehicles displaying L plates is 45 mph (72km/h), except goods vehicles, buses and coaches on a motorway.

Laws MV(DL)R reg 12, RTO 1981 Art 19 & MV(SLRE)R reg 2

You **MUST** pass the theory test (if one is required) and then a practical driving test for the category of vehicle you wish to drive before driving unaccompanied.

Law MV(DL)R reg 30

Restricted drivers

After passing the driving test for a motor car or a motorcycle, you must display amber R plates for a period of one year from the date of passing the test. The plates **MUST** conform to legal specifications and **MUST** be clearly visible to others from in front of the vehicle and from behind. Plates should be removed or covered when not being driven by a restricted driver.

The maximum permitted speed for a motor car or category A1 motorcycle displaying R plates is 45 mph (72km/h), whether or not the vehicle is being driven by a restricted driver. The speed restriction does not apply to A2 or A motorcycles, although R plates must be displayed for the first year after passing the test.

Laws RTO 1981 Art 19A & MV(PR)R

4. The road user and the law

Road traffic law

The following list can be found abbreviated throughout the Code. It is not intended to be a comprehensive guide, but a guide to some of the important points of law. For the precise wording of the law, please refer to the various Orders and Regulations (as amended) indicated in the Code. Abbreviations are listed as follows.

Most of the provisions apply on all roads throughout Northern Ireland. A road includes a public road, any part of a public road and any bridges or tunnels over or through which a public road passes, and any street, carriageway, highway or roadway to which the public has access (RTO 1995 Art 2). It is important to note that references to 'road' therefore generally include footways, footpaths, and cycle tracks and many roadways and driveways on private land (including many car parks). In most cases, the law will apply to them and there may be additional rules for particular paths or ways. Some serious driving offences, including drink-driving offences, also apply to all public places, for example public car parks.

Chronically Sick & Disabled Persons (NI) Act 1978	CSPDA
Criminal Justice (NI) Order 1994	CJO
Horses (Protective Headgear for Young Riders) (NI) Order 1990	H(PHYR)O
Horses (Protective Headgear for Young Riders) Regulations (NI) 1992	H(PHYR)R
Litter (NI) Order 1994	LO
Motor Cycles (Eye Protectors) Regulations (NI) 2004	MC(EP)R
Motor Cycles (Protective Headgear) Regulations (NI) 1999	MC(PH)R
Motor Vehicles (Construction & Use) Regulations (NI) 1999	CUR
Motor Vehicles (Construction & Use) (Amendment No.5) Regulations (NI) 2003	CU(A)R
Motor Vehicles (Constructions & Use) (Amendment) Regulations (NI) 2005	CU(A)R
Motor Vehicles (Driving Licences) Regulations (NI) 1996	MV(DL)R
Motor Vehicles (Driving Licences) (Amendment) Regulations (NI) 2003 (4 sets of Regulations)	MVDL(A)R
Motor Vehicles (Invalid Carriages) Regulations (NI) 1999	MV(IC)R
Motor Vehicles (Prescribed Restrictions) Regulations (NI) 1996	MV(PR)R
Motor Vehicles (Speed Limits) Regulations (NI) 1989	MV(SL)R
Motor Vehicles (Speed Limit Restriction) (Exemption) Regulations (NI) 1998	MV(SLRE)R
Motor Vehicles (Wearing of Seat Belts) Regulations (NI) 1993	MV(WSB)R
Motor Vehicles (Wearing of Seat Belts by Children in Front Seats) Regulations (NI) 1993 and 2007	MV(WSBCFS)R
Motor Vehicles (Wearing of Seat Belts) (Amendment) Regulations (NI) 2007 and 2008	MV(WSB)(A)R
Motorways Traffic Regulations (NI) 2008	MTR
Road Traffic Act 1984, 1988 or 1991 (as indicated)	RTA
Road Traffic (New Drivers) (NI) Order 1998	RT(ND)O
Road Traffic (NI) Order 1981, 1995 or 2007 (as indicated)	RTO
Road Traffic Offenders (NI) Order 1996	RTOO
Road Traffic Regulation (NI) Order 1997	RTRO
Road Vehicles (Display of Registration Marks) Regulations 2001	RV(DRM)R
Road Vehicles Lighting Regulations (NI) 2000	RVLR
Road Vehicles Lighting (Amendment) Regulations (NI) 2007	RVL(A)R
Road Vehicles (Registration & Licensing) Regulations 2002	RV(R&L)R
Road Vehicles (Traffic) Regulations 1933	RV(T)R
Roads (NI) Order 1993	RO
Roads (Restriction of Waiting) Order (NI) 1982	R(RW)O
Smoke-Free (Exemptions, Vehicles, Penalties & Discounted Amounts) Regulations (NI) 2007	SF(EVPDA)R
Smoking (NI) Order 2006	SO
Traffic Management Act 2004	TMA
Traffic Signs Regulations (NI) 1997	TSR
Vehicle Excise and Registration Act 1994	VERA
Zebra Pelican & Puffin Pedestrian Crossing Regulations (NI) 2006	PCR

Orders and regulations from 1988 can be viewed on The National Archives website (www.legislation.gov.uk). Orders and regulations prior to 1988 are only available in their original print format which can be obtained from The Stationery Office as detailed inside the back cover.

5. Penalties

Parliament sets the maximum penalties for road traffic offences. The seriousness of the offence is reflected in the maximum penalty. It is for the courts to decide what sentence to impose according to circumstances.

The penalty table on page 126 indicates some of the main offences and the associated penalties. There is a wide range of other more specific offences which, for the sake of simplicity, are not shown here. The penalty points and disqualification system is described below.

Penalty points and disqualifications

The penalty points system is intended to deter drivers and motorcyclists from following unsafe motoring practices. Certain non-motoring offences, e.g. failure to rectify vehicle defects, can also attract penalty points. The court **MUST** order points to be endorsed on the licence according to the fixed number or the range set by Parliament. The accumulation of penalty points acts as a warning to drivers that they risk disqualification if further offences are committed.

Law RTOO Arts 49 & 50

A driver or motorcyclist who accumulates 12 or more penalty points within a three-year period must be disqualified. This will be for a minimum period of six months, or longer if the driver or motorcyclist has previously been disqualified.

Law RTOO Art 40

For every offence which carries penalty points the court has a discretionary power to order the licence holder to be disqualified. This may be for any period the court thinks fit, but will usually be between a week and a few months.

In the case of serious offences, such as dangerous driving and drink-driving, the court **MUST** order disqualification. The minimum period is 12 months, but for repeat offenders or where the alcohol level is high, it may be longer. For example, a second drink-drive offence in the space of 10 years will be result in a minimum of three years' disqualification.

Law RTOO Art 35

Furthermore, in some serious cases, the court **MUST** (in addition to imposing a fixed period of disqualification) order the offender to be disqualified until they pass a driving test. In other cases the court has a discretionary power to order such disqualification.

Penalty Table

Offence	Maximum Penalties — Imprisonment	Fine	Disqualification	Penalty Points
* Causing deaths, or grievous bodily injury by dangerous driving	14 years	Unlimited	Obligatory - 2 years minimum	3-11 (if exceptionally not disqualified)
*Dangerous driving	5 years	Unlimited	Obligatory	3-11 (if exceptionally not disqualified)
* Causing death, or grievous bodily injury by careless driving when under the influence of drink or drugs	14 years	Unlimited	Obligatory - 2 years minimum	3-11 (if exceptionally not disqualified)
Aggravated vehicle taking causing death or grievous bodily injury	14 years	Unlimited	Obligatory	3-11
Careless and inconsiderate driving	-	£5,000	Discretionary	3-9
** Driving while unfit through drink or drugs or with excess alcohol; or failing to provide a specimen for analysis	6 months	£5,000	Obligatory	3-11 (if exceptionally not disqualified)
Failing to stop after an accident (collision) or failing to report an accident (collision)	6 months	£5,000	Discretionary	5-10
Driving when disqualified	2 years	Unlimited	Discretionary	6
Causing death or grievous bodily injury by careless or inconsiderate driving	5 years	Unlimited	Obligatory	3-11
Driving without insurance	6 months	£5,000	Discretionary	6-8
Causing death or grievous bodily injury by driving unlicensed, uninsured or while disqualified	2 years	Unlimited	Obligatory	3-11
Speeding	-	£1,000 (£2,500 for motorway offences)	Discretionary	3-6 or 3 (fixed penalty)
Traffic light offences	-	£1,000	Discretionary	3
No MOT certificate	-	£1,000	-	-
Seat belt offences	-	£500	-	3
Dangerous cycling	-	£2,500	-	-
Careless cycling	-	£1,000	-	-
Failing to identify driver of a vehicle	-	£1,000	Discretionary	6

* Where a court disqualifies a person on conviction for one of these offences, it must order an extended retest and for those offences marked
** it must order an ordinary retest. The courts also have discretion to order a retest for any other offence which carries obligatory endorsement, an extended retest where disqualification is for repeated offences and an ordinary retest in any other case.

The test may be of ordinary or extended length according to the nature of the offence.

Law RTOO Art 41

New drivers. Special rules as set out below apply for a period of two years from the date of passing their first driving test, to drivers and motorcyclists from

- the UK, EU/EEA, the Isle of Man, the Channel Islands or Gibraltar who passed their first driving test in any of those countries;
- other foreign countries who have to pass a UK driving test to gain a UK licence, in which case the UK driving licence is treated as their first driving test; and
- other foreign countries who (without needing a test) exchanged their licence for a UK licence and subsequently passed a UK driving test to drive another type of vehicle, in which case the UK driving test is treated as their first driving test. For example a driver who exchanges a foreign licence (car) for a UK licence (car) and who later passes a test to drive another type of vehicle (e.g an LGV) will be subject to the special rules.

Where a person subject to the special rules accumulates six or more penalty points before the end of the two-year period (including any points acquired before passing the test), their licence will be revoked automatically. To regain the licence they must reapply for a provisional licence and may drive only as a learner until they pass a further driving test (also see Annex 8 – Safety code for new drivers).

Law RT(ND)O

Note. This applies even if they pay for offences by fixed penalty. Drivers in the first group (UK, EU/EEA etc.), who already have a full licence for one type of vehicle are not affected by the special rules if they later pass a test to drive another type of vehicle.

Other consequences of offending
Where an offence is punishable by imprisonment, the vehicle used to commit the offence may be confiscated.

Law CJO Art 11

In addition to the penalties a court may decide to impose, the cost of insurance is likely to rise considerably following conviction for a serious driving offence. This is because insurance companies consider such drivers are more likely to have a collision.

Drivers disqualified for alcohol related motoring offences twice within 10 years, or once if they are over two and a half times the legal limit, or those who refused to give a specimen, also have to satisfy Driver and Vehicle Agency's Medical Branch that they do not have an alcohol problem and are otherwise fit to drive before a provisional licence is issued after the period of disqualification. Persistent misuse of drugs or alcohol may lead to the withdrawal of a driving licence.

6. Vehicle maintenance, safety and security

Vehicle maintenance

Take special care that lights, brakes, steering, exhaust system, seat belts, demisters, wipers and washers are all working. Also

- lights, indicators, reflectors and number plates **MUST** be kept clean and clear
- windscreen and windows **MUST** be kept clean and free from obstructions to vision
- lights **MUST** be properly adjusted to prevent dazzling other road users. Extra attention needs to be paid to this if the vehicle is heavily loaded
- exhaust emissions **MUST NOT** exceed prescribed levels
- ensure your seat, seat belt, head restraint and mirrors are adjusted correctly before you drive
- ensure that items of luggage are securely stowed.

Laws RVLR regs 26 & 30, & CUR regs 35 & 74

Warning displays. Make sure that you understand the meaning of all warning displays on the vehicle instrument panel. Do not ignore warning signs; they could indicate a dangerous fault developing.

- When you turn the ignition key, warning lights will be illuminated but will go out when the engine starts (except the handbrake warning light). If they do not, or if they come on while you are driving, stop and investigate the problem, as there could be a serious fault.
- If the charge warning light comes on while you are driving, it may mean that the battery isn't charging. This must also be checked as soon as possible to avoid loss of power to lights and other electrical systems.

Window tints. You **MUST NOT** use a vehicle with excessively dark tinting fitted to the windscreen, or to the glass in any front window to either side of the driver. Window tinting applied during manufacture complies with the visual light transmittance (VLT) standards. There are no VLT limits for rear windscreens or rear passenger windows.

Laws RTO 1995 Art 58, CUR reg 37 & CU(A)R 2005

Tyres. Tyres **MUST** be correctly inflated to the vehicle manufacturer's specification for the load being carried. Always refer to the vehicle's handbook or data. Tyres should also be free from certain cuts or other defects.

Cars, light vans and light trailers MUST have a tread depth of at least 1.6mm across the central three-quarters of the breadth of the tread and around the entire circumference.

Motorcycles, large vehicles and passenger-carrying vehicles MUST have a tread depth of at least 1mm across three-quarters of the breadth of the tread and in a continuous band around the entire circumference.

Mopeds should have visible tread.

Be aware that some vehicle defects can attract penalty points.

Law CUR reg 32

If a tyre bursts while you are driving, try to keep control of your vehicle. Grip the steering wheel firmly and allow the vehicle to roll to a stop at the side of the road.

If you have a flat tyre, stop as soon as it is safe to do so. Only change the tyre if you can do so without putting yourself or others at risk – otherwise call a breakdown service.

Tyre pressures. Check weekly. Do this before your journey, when tyres are cold. Warm or hot tyres may give a misleading reading.

Your brakes and steering will be adversely affected by under-inflated or over-inflated tyres. Excessive or uneven tyre wear may be caused by faults in the braking or suspensions systems, or wheels which are out of alignment. Have these faults corrected as soon as possible.

Spacesaver tyres, often referred to as 'get you home tyres', are speed or distance rated. Advice on their use can be found on the tyre or in the vehicle handbook.

Run flat tyres, which should only be used in conjunction with a tyre pressure monitoring system, enable vehicles to continue at reduced speeds for a limited distance following a puncture. Advice on their use can be found in the vehicle handbook.

Fluid levels. Check the fluid levels in your vehicle at least weekly. Low brake fluid may result in brake failure and a collision. Make sure you recognise the low fluid warning lights if your vehicle has them fitted.

Before winter. Ensure that the battery is well maintained and that there are appropriate anti-freeze agents in your radiator and windscreen bottle.

Other problems. If your vehicle

- pulls to one side when braking, it is most likely to be a brake fault or incorrectly inflated tyres. Consult a garage or mechanic immediately
- continues to bounce after pushing down on the front or rear, its shock absorbers are worn. Worn shock absorbers can seriously affect the operation of a vehicle and should be replaced
- smells of anything unusual such as burning rubber, petrol or an electrical fault; investigate immediately. Do not risk a fire.

Overheated engines or fire. Most engines are water-cooled. If your engine overheats you should wait until it has cooled naturally. Only then remove the coolant filler cap and add water or other coolant.

If your vehicle catches fire, get the occupants out of the vehicle quickly and to a safe place. Do not attempt to extinguish a fire in the engine compartment, as opening the bonnet will make the fire flare. Call the Fire and Rescue Service.

Petrol stations/fuel tank/fuel leaks. Ensure that, when filling up your vehicle's tank or any fuel cans you are carrying, you do not spill fuel on the forecourt. Any spilled fuel should be immediately reported to the petrol station attendant. Diesel spillage is dangerous to other road users, particularly motorcyclists, as it will significantly reduce the level of grip between the tyres and the road surface. Double-check for fuel leaks and make sure that

- you do not overfill your fuel tank
- the fuel cap is fastened securely
- the seal in the cap is not torn, perished or missing
- there is no visual damage to the cap or the fuel tank.

Emergency fuel caps, if fitted, should form a good seal.

Never smoke, or use a mobile phone, on the forecourt of petrol stations as these are major fire risks and could cause an explosion.

Vehicle security
When you leave your vehicle you should

- remove the ignition key and engage the steering lock
- lock the car, even if you only leave it for a few minutes
- close the windows completely
- never leave children or pets in an unventilated car
- take all contents with you, or lock them in the boot. Remember a potential thief might assume a carrier bag contains valuables
- never leave vehicle documents in the car.

For extra security fit an anti-theft device such as an alarm or immobiliser. If you are buying a new car it is a good idea to check the level of built-in security features. Consider having your registration number etched on all your car windows. This is a cheap and effective deterrent to professional thieves.

7. First aid on the road

The following information was compiled with the assistance of St John Ambulance, the British Heart Foundation and the British Red Cross. It is intended as a general guide for those without first aid training but should not be considered a substitute for proper training. Any first aid given at the scene of an incident should be looked on only as a temporary measure until the emergency services arrive.

1. Deal with danger
Further collisions and fire are the main dangers following a crash. Approach any vehicle involved with care, watching out for spilt oil or broken glass. Switch off all engines and, if possible, warn other traffic. If you have a vehicle, switch on your hazard warning lights. Stop anyone from smoking, and put on the gloves from your first aid kit if you have one.

2. Get help

If you can do so safely, try to get the assistance of bystanders. Get someone to call the appropriate emergency services on 999 or 112 as soon as possible. They'll need to know the exact location of the incident (including the direction of traffic, eg northbound) and the number of vehicles involved. Try to give information about the condition of any casualties, eg if anyone is having difficulty breathing, is bleeding heavily, is trapped in a vehicle or does not respond when spoken to.

3. Help those involved

DO NOT move casualties from their vehicles unless there is the threat of further danger. **DO NOT** remove a motorcyclist's helmet unless it is essential. **DO** try to keep casualties warm, dry and as comfortable as you can. **DO** give reassurance confidently and try not to leave them alone or let them wander into the path of other traffic. **DO NOT** give them anything to eat or drink.

4. Provide emergency care

Remember the letters **DR A B C**.

D – Danger Check that it is safe to approach.

R – Response Try to get a response by gently shaking the casualty's shoulders and asking loudly 'Are you all right?' If they respond, check for injuries.

A – Airway If there is no response, open the casualty's airway by placing your fingers under their chin and lifting it forward.

> If the casualty is unconscious and breathing, place them in the recovery position until medical help arrives

B – Breathing Check that the casualty is breathing normally. Look for chest movements, look and listen for breathing, and feel for breath on your cheek.

If there are no signs of breathing, start CPR. Interlock your fingers, place them in the centre of the casualty's chest and press down hard and fast – around 5–6 centimetres and about twice a second. You may only need one hand for a child and shouldn't press down as far. For infants, use two fingers in the middle of the chest and press down about a third of the chest depth. Don't stop until the casualty starts breathing again or a medical professional takes over.

C – Circulation If the casualty is responsive and breathing, check for signs of bleeding. Protect yourself from exposure to blood and check for anything that may be in the wound, such as glass. Don't remove anything that's stuck in the wound. Taking care not to press on the object, build up padding on either side of the object. If nothing is embedded, apply firm pressure over the wound to stem the flow of blood. As soon as practical, fasten a pad to the wound with a bandage or length of cloth. Use the cleanest material available.

Burns. Put out any flames, taking care for your own safety. Cool the burn for at least 20 minutes with plenty of clean, cool water. Cover the burn with cling film if available. Don't try to remove anything that's sticking to the burn.

5. Be prepared

Always carry a first aid kit – you might never need it, but it could save a life. Learn first aid – you can get training from a qualified organisation such as the local ambulance services, St John Ambulance, the Order of Malta Ambulance Corps, the British Red Cross or any suitable qualified body (see page 135 for contact details).

8. Safety code for new drivers

Once you have passed the driving test you will be able to drive on your own. This will provide you with lots of opportunities but you need to remain safe. Even though you have shown you have the skills you need to drive safely, many newly qualified drivers lack experience. You need to continue to develop your skills, especially anticipating other road users' behaviour to avoid having a collision. As many as one new driver in five has some kind of collision in their first year of driving. This code provides advice to help you get through the first 12 months after passing the driving test, when you are vulnerable, as safely as possible.

- Many of the worst collisions happen at night. Between midnight and 6.00 am is a time of high risk for new drivers. Avoid driving then unless it's really necessary.
- If you are driving with passengers, you are responsible for their safety. Don't let them distract you or encourage you to take risks. Tell your passengers that you need to concentrate if you are to get to your destination safely.
- Never show off or try to compete with other drivers, particularly if they are driving badly.
- Don't drive if you have consumed any alcohol or taken drugs. Even over-the-counter medicines can affect your ability to drive safely – read the label to see if they may affect your driving.
- Make sure everyone in the car is wearing a seat belt throughout the journey.
- Keep your speed down – many serious collisions happen because the driver loses control, particularly on bends.
- Most new drivers have no experience of driving high-powered or sporty cars. Unless you have learnt to drive in such a vehicle you need to get plenty of experience driving on your own before driving a more powerful car.
- Driving while uninsured is an offence. See Annex 3 for information on types of insurance cover.

REMEMBER that under the New Drivers Order you will have your licence revoked if you get six penalty points on your licence within two years of passing your first driving tests. You will need to pass both the theory and practical tests again to get back your full licence.

You could consider taking further training or obtaining an advanced driving qualification which could save you money on your insurance as well as helping you reduce your risk of being involved in a collision. There are three ways to find out more:

- **internet** www.nidirect.gov.uk/articles/new-drivers
- **telephone** DfI Promotion and Outreach Branch
  0300 200 7838
- **email** safeandsustainabletravel@infrastructure-ni.gov.uk

Other information

Metric conversions

The conversions given throughout *The Highway Code* are rounded, but a detailed conversion chart is shown below.

Miles	Kilometres	Miles	Kilometres
1.00	1.61	40.00	64.37
5.00	8.05	45.00	72.42
10.00	16.09	50.00	80.47
15.00	24.14	55.00	88.51
20.00	32.19	60.00	96.56
25.00	40.23	65.00	104.60
30.00	48.28	70.00	112.65
35.00	56.33		

Useful websites

- www.nidirect.gov.uk
- www.sja.org.uk (St John Ambulance)
- www.orderofmaltaireland.org (Order of Malta Ambulance Corps)
- www.redcross.org.uk (British Red Cross)
- www.nidirect.gov.uk/information-and-services/motoring
- www.trafficwatchni.com/twni/roadworks
- www.psni.police.uk
- www.rsa.ie
- www.tii.ie
- www.roadsafeni.com
- www.gov.uk/government/organisations/driver-and-vehicle-licensing-agency
- www.sharetheroadtozero.com

Further reading

Best practice
Further information about good driving and riding practice can be found in the Driver and Vehicle Standards Agency books *The Official DVSA Guide to Driving – the essential skills* and *The Official DVSA Guide to Riding – the essential skills*. Information specifically for drivers of large vehicles can be found in *The Official DVSA Guide to Driving Goods Vehicles and The Official DVSA Guide to Driving Buses and Coaches*.

The Blue Badge Scheme
Information on this scheme can be found at www.nidirect.gov.uk/information-and-services/motoring-and-transport/blue-badge-scheme

Code of Practice for Horse-Drawn Vehicles
The Code of Practice is available from the Department for Transport, International Vehicle Standards, Great Minster House, 33 Horseferry Road, London SW1P 4DR. Tel. 0300 330 3000

www.gov.uk/government/publications/code-of-practice-for-horse-drawn-vehicles

Appendix

Roundabouts are safe and simple if you know and use these rules
Many drivers are satisfied with their own use of roundabouts, but believe others do it all wrong! Before criticising other drivers' roundabout behaviour, check your knowledge of the rules.

Why roundabouts?
When used properly, roundabouts can smooth traffic flow at busy junctions. Vehicles can enter and leave roundabouts by different roads with less inconvenience or danger. They are really circular, clockwise one-way traffic systems enabling several traffic streams to mix.

The rules for using roundabouts
Give way: the most important rule – when entering a roundabout, give way to traffic on the roundabout, unless road markings or signs say otherwise. If the way is clear keep moving. Stopping at a clear roundabout slows traffic and can cause frustrating delays.

A roundabout entrance is usually marked by a single broken line across the road. Sometimes you may find other markings. At some roundabouts one traffic lane might be allowed to flow free; there will be road markings or signs to show this.

Speed: approach so that you can stop and give way if necessary. Approaching too fast could make other drivers on the roundabout think that you are going to drive in front of them. They could brake or swerve and perhaps cause a collision. If you approach too fast and brake hard at a roundabout entrance you could also cause a collision by panicking a following driver who might skid into the back of your vehicle.

On the roundabout, you should drive according to road, weather and traffic conditions as well as the road-holding qualities of your vehicle.

Position and signals: Being correctly positioned and signalling clearly in good time helps other road users. Knowing and following the rules improves traffic flow and safety at roundabouts.

While this appendix provides general advice, other factors such as signs, road markings and the position and type of other vehicles can influence the choice of lane. Where there are signs or road markings which indicate appropriate lanes, these should assume priority over the following procedures.

Correct roundabout procedure

Imagine that you are approaching a busy roundabout with six converging roads. Follow the advice in the diagrams. Treat the roundabout as if it were a clock face. All movement on roundabouts is clockwise.

Always assume that your approach is from the six o'clock position. Approach at the correct speed and in the right gear. Always signal your intentions clearly. If there is no traffic at or on the roundabout you may take the shortest and most convenient route through it. Cancel your signal after leaving the roundabout.

Now that you know the rules, show a good example to other drivers by following them every time. They may even copy your driving style and do it right too!

1. **Taking the first exit (b) at 8 o'clock**

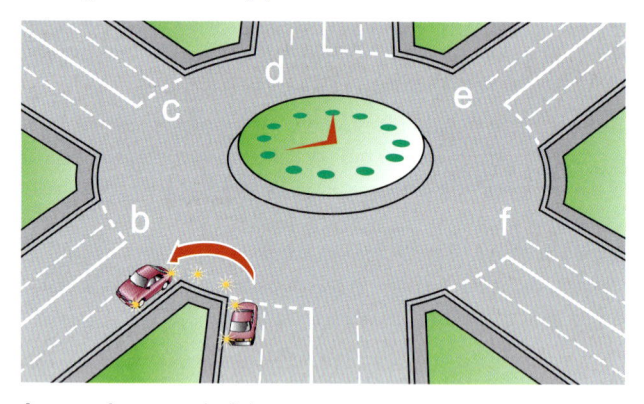

Approach	Left lane
Signal	All-round observation and left-turn indicator on approach
On roundabout	Keep in left lane
Exit	Check mirrors before leaving roundabout and keep left-turn indicator going until just after leaving roundabout

2. **Taking the second exit (c) at 10 o'clock**

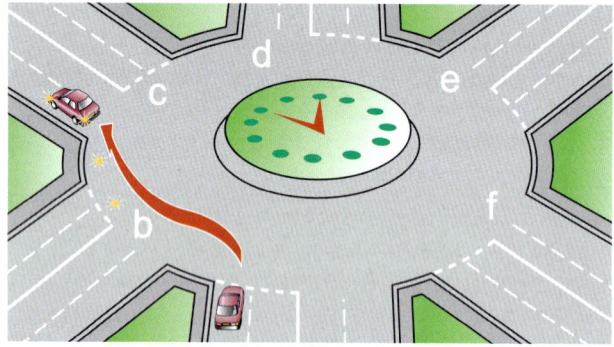

Approach	Left lane
Signal	All-round observation; no approach signal
On roundabout	Keep in left lane
Exit	Check mirrors and indicate left when you have passed exit (b) before the one you want to take (c)

3. Taking the third exit (d) at 12 o'clock

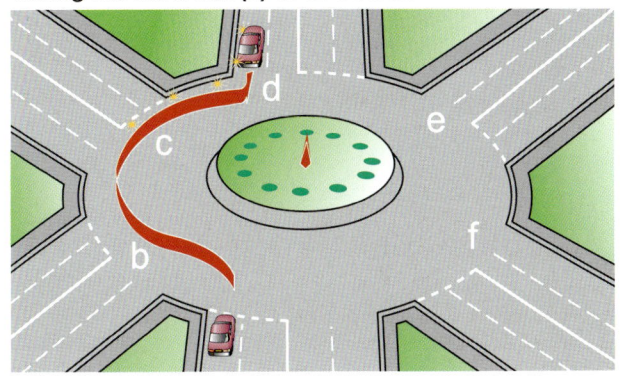

Approach	Left lane
Signal	No approach signal
On roundabout	Keep in left lane (use right lane if approach was in right lane)
Exit	Check mirrors and indicate left when you have passed exit (c) before the one you want to take (d)

4. Taking the fourth exit (2) at 2 o'clock

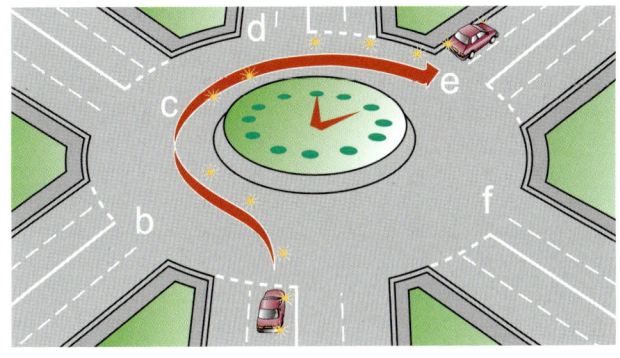

Approach	Right lane
Signal	All-round observation and indicate right on approach
On roundabout	Keep in right lane near centre of roundabout; keep right-turn indicator going
Exit	Check mirrors and change to left-turn indicator when you have passed exit (d) before the one you want to take (e). Check mirrors, glance over left shoulder and ease into left lane for exit (e)

5. Taking the fifth exit (f) at 4 o'clock

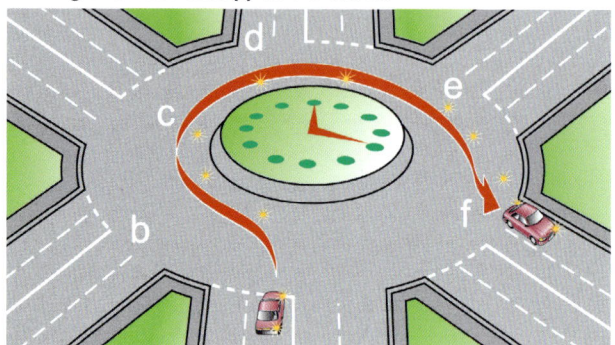

Approach	Right lane
Signal	All-round observation and indicate right on approach
On roundabout	Keep in right lane near centre of roundabout; keep right-turn indicator going
Exit	Check mirrors and change to left-turn indicator when you have passed exit (e) before the one you want to take (f). Check mirrors, glance over left shoulder and ease into left lane for exit (f)

Index

References are to rule numbers, except those numbers in blue italics, which are page numbers

A

ABS *see* Braking/brakes
Active Traffic Management (ATM) signs 269
Advanced stop lines 61, 71, 178
Airbags 101
Alcohol 68, 95, *125-128*
Animals 47-58, 214-215, 286
 horses 47-56, 163, 187, 214-215, 286
 level crossings 294
 motorways 253, 275
Annexes *118-134*
Arm signals 53, 55, 67, 74, 103, *103-105*
Appendix *136-140*
Attitude 147

B

Baby seats *see* Rear-facing baby seats
Battery *130*
Bell *118*
Bends 2, 125, 146, 160, 166, 231, 243
Blind spots 159, 161, 202, 267
Blue Badge scheme 45, *136*
Box junctions 174, *116*
Brake warning lights 103, 235, *103*
Braking/brakes 117-122, 231, 237, *128*
 ABS braking 120
 condition of *128, 129-130*
Breakdowns 274
 level crossings 299
 motorways 274-277
Bright sunlight *see* Dazzle
Bus lanes 141, 240
 crossing 12, 183
 cyclists 65
 one-way streets 11, 143
 overtaking 165
 parking 240
 turning 183
Bus stops 243
 give way 223
 overtaking 167
 pedestrians 206, 223, 243
 school 209
Buses 223, 265
 board/alight 32
 overtaking 65, 167
 school 209

C

Car phones *see* Mobile phones
Caravans 98, 160, 250, 265
Central islands 7, 20, 28, 30, 197, 243
Changing lanes 133, 134, 151
Chicanes 153
Child locks 102
Child restraints 99-100, 102
Children
 cars 99-100, 102, *131*
 Green Cross Code 7, 30
 horses 215
 on motorways 275
 other goods vehicles 99-100, 102
 parking 239
 pedestrian crossings 18, 29

pedestrians 7, 202, 204-210, 306
vans 99-100, 102
young 4
Clearways 240, *107*
Climbing/crawler lane 139
Clothing
 cyclists 59
 drivers 97, 228
 horse riders 49
 motorcyclists 83-84, 86-87
 pedestrians 3, 5, 17, 58
Coasting 122
Concentration 148-150, 288
Consideration 144, 147
Conspicuity
 cyclists 59-60
 horse-drawn vehicles 48
 horse riders 49-50
 motorcyclists 86-87
 pedestrians 3, 5, 17, 58
Contraflow systems 290
Controlled crossings 7, 22-30, 79-82, 196-199
Controlled parking zones 238, 245
Controls 97
Country roads 154
Courtesy 147
Crossing the road 7-35
 cyclists 79-82
Crossings *see* Pedestrian crossings
Crossroads (unmarked) 146
Cruise control 150
Cycle lanes and tracks
 cyclists 61-63, 65
 dogs 56
 drivers 140
 horse riders 54
 parking 140, 240
 pedestrians 11-13, 62, 66
 turning 183

Cycle maintenance/choice *118*
Cycle-only crossing 81
Cyclists and cycling 59-82, 211-213, 253
 junctions 72-75, 170, 177-178, 180, 182-183, 211
 overtaking/clearance 65, 129, 160, 163, 212, 232
 pedestrians 13, 62, 66
 rear observation 67, 212
 roundabouts 76-78, 187
 routes 61-63, 65
 traffic lights 69, 71, 79-82, 177-178
 trams 306
 turning 74, 212

D

Dangerous goods 284-285
Dazzle 93, 115, 236-237
Decriminalised Parking *84*
Demisters 229, 235, *128*
Diagonal stripes/chevrons 130, *114*
Direction indicators *see* Signals
Disabled 204, 207
 cyclists 62
 drivers on motorway 253, 278
 pedestrian crossings 26
 vehicles for 36-46, 220, 239, 241, 250
Distractions 148-150
Documents 286-287, *120-123*
Dogs (including guide dogs) 56-57, 207
Double white lines 128-129, 165, 240, *114*
Drinking and driving 68, 95, *125-128*

Driver and Vehicle Agency Enforcement Officer
  signals and livery **105**
  stopping powers 107
Driving, general advice 144-156
Driving licence **118-122**
Drugs/medicine 68, 96
Dual carriageways
  crossing/turning 137, 173
  cyclists 75
  three-lane 138
  two-lane 137
Dull weather 115

E

Electric vehicles 224
Emergency telephones 275, 280, 283
Emergency vehicles 31, 219, 281
Environmental issues 123
Equestrian Crossings 27, 79, 199
Exhaust systems **128**
Eyesight/vision 92-94

F

Fatigue 91, 237, 262
Filter lights 177
Fire **130**
First aid 283, **131-133**
Fitness to drive 90-91
Flashing amber beacons 220, 225
Flashing headlights 60, 110-111
Flashing signals
  emergency 31, 219, 281
  headlights 110, 111
  level crossings 293
  motorways 257-258, 270
  police 31, 106, 219, 281
  school 208
  slow-moving vehicles 220, 225
  tramways 33
Fluorescent/reflective clothing
  breakdowns 274
  cyclists 59
  horse riders 50
  motorcyclists 86-87
  pedestrians 3, 5, 17
Fog 234-236
  lights 114, 226, 236
  motorways 235, 255, 260
  parking 251
Footways/footpaths
  cyclists 13, 62, 64, 70
  drivers 145
  horses 54
  parking 244
  pedestrians 1-2, 4, 13
  prohibited vehicles 157-158
  repairs 35

G

Give way
  junctions 172, 183, 185, 189, 206
  motorways 259
Go-peds *see* Prohibited vehicles
Green Cross Code 7, 30

H

Hard shoulder *see* Motorways
Hazard warning lights 116, 274, 277-278, 283
Hazard warning plates 284, **117**
Head restraints 97, **128**
Headlamps and headlights 113-115, 226, 235, 239
  motorcycle 87
Headlight flashing 110-111
Helmets
  cyclists 59
  horse riders 49

143

incidents 283, *132*
motorcyclists 83, 86, 283, *132*
High-occupancy vehicle lanes (HOVs) 142, *112*
Hills
control 160
parking 243, 252
Home zones 206, 218
Horn 112, 214
Horse-drawn vehicles 47-48, 215, *136*
Horse riders 49-55, 163, 187, 214, 215, 253
Hot weather 237
HOVs *see* High-occupancy vehicle lanes

I

Ice cream vans 206
Icy weather 126, 195, 213, 228-231, 260
In-vehicle technology 149-150
Incident support vehicles 219
Incidents 281-287, *131-133*
dangerous goods 284-285
documentation 286-287
first aid 283, *131-133*
flashing lights 281
level crossing 299
motorway 283
warning signs 281
Inexperienced drivers 204, 217, *133-134*
Insurance 287, *121-122*
Islands 7, 20, 28, 30, 197, 243

J

Junctions *see* Road junctions

L

L plates *118-120, 123*

Lamps and lights
conditions/maintenance 113, 229, *118, 128*
cyclists 60
horses 51
pedestrians 5, 58
vehicles 113-116, 249-251, 274
see also Headlamps and headlights
Lane discipline 133-143, 288
dual carriageways 137-138
motorways 263-265
multi-lane carriageways 133
one-way streets 143
roundabouts 184-187
single carriageways 135
Lane dividers 131, *114*
Large vehicles 126, 160, 164, 221-222, 233, 294
see also Long/large vehicles
Lay-bys 249-250
Learner drivers 204, 217, 253, *122-123*
Level crossings 34, 54, 82, 167, 243, 291-299
Lighting requirements 5, 43, 48, 60, 113-115, 226, 229, 235-236
Lights *see* Headlamps and headlights, Lamps and lights
Lines and lanes 127-132, 136-143, 184-185, *114*
see also Traffic signs/road markings
Littering from vehicles 147
Loading and unloading 246-247
Loads 98, 250
Long/large vehicles
cyclists 73, 78
junctions 170, 173
road works 288
roundabouts 78, 187-188

trams 300-307
see also Large vehicles

M

Maintenance of vehicles *128-131*
Manoeuvring 159-190, 200-203
 large vehicles 221
 motorcycles 88
Medicines 68, 96
Merging in turn 134, 288
Metric conversion table *135*
Miniature motorcycles (mini-motos) *see* Prohibited vehicles
Mini-roundabouts 188-190
Mirrors 97, 161, 184, 202, 229, 288-289, *128*
 changing lanes 133
 fog 234-235
 motorways 254, 267
 moving off 97, 159
 overtaking 163, 267
 turning 179-180, 182
Mobile phones 97, 149, 270, 275, 278, 283, 285, *131*
MOT *121*
Motorcycle licence *118-120*
Motorcyclists 83-98, 160, 211-213, 232-233, 250, 253, 306
 conspicuity 86-87
 junctions 88, 170, 180, 182, 211-213
 learners 204, 217, 253, *118-120*
 night riding 87
 overall stopping distance 126, 227, 230, 235, 260
 overtaking 88, 163, 230
 rear observation 88, 212
 roundabouts 187
 turning 88
 winter 230, *130*
Motor tricycles *see* Prohibited vehicles
Motorways 253-273
 breakdowns 274-277
 contraflow systems 290
 emergency telephones 275, 283
 fog 234
 hard shoulder 275, 290
 obstructions 279-280
 pedestrians 6
 road works 288
 signals/signs/flashing lights 255-258, 272, 281
 stopping and parking 91, 240
 studs 132
Moving off 159

N

Narrow/winding roads *see* Country roads
Navigation systems 150
New Drivers *127, 133-134*
Night
 animals 51, 58
 cyclists 60
 driving 94
 lights *see* Lamps and lights
 motorways 267
 overtaking 163
 parking 248-251
 pedestrians 3, 5, 17
 speed 125

O

Obstructions 279-280
 cyclists 67, 70
 lines/lanes 288-289
 motorways 280
 vehicles 146, 163, 242
Older drivers 216

Older pedestrians 62, 204, 207
One-way streets 143
  crossing 11
  horses 53
Organised walks 5
Other stopping procedures 107-108
Overhead electric lines 292, 307
Overtaking 135, 160, 162-169, 230
  animals 163, 214-215
  before overtaking 162
  being overtaken 168-169
  bus lanes 165
  crossings 165, 191
  cyclists 65, 67, 129, 160, 163, 211-212, 232
  dual carriageways 137-138
  horse riders 215
  long vehicles 160, 164, 169
  motorcyclists 88, 163, 211-212, 230
  motorways 267-268
  queues 163, 288
  single-track roads 155
  trams 167, 301, 303

P

Parked vehicles
  Green Cross Code 7
  pedestrians 7, 14, 193, 206
Parking 238-252, 302
  at night 248-250
  bicycles 70
  goods vehicles 246-247
  hazard warning lights 116
  level crossings 291
  motorways 91, 240
  pedestrian crossings 191
  single-track roads 156
Passengers, carriage of 99, 275
  by cyclists 68
  by horse riders 53
  by learners *120*
  by motorcyclists 85, *120*
Passing places 155-156
Pavements **see** Footways/footpaths
Pedestrian crossings 18-30, 191-199, 240
  controlled 7, 21-28, 80, 196-199
  equestrian 27, 79
  level 34
  pelican 7, 22, 24, 79, 196-198
  puffin 7, 23-24, 79, 199
  staggered 28
  toucan 7, 25-26, 80, 199
  traffic lights 21
  zebra 7, 19-20, 79, 195
Pedestrians 1-35, 125, 146, 152, 154, 202, 204-210, 223, 244
  blind/deaf/older 26, 62, 66, 204, 207, 244
  cyclists 13, 62, 66
  junctions 8, 170, 180, 206
  motorways 6, 253, 271
  safety 1, 204-210, 239
  safety barriers 9
  tramways 33, 206, 223, 304
Pelican crossings 22, 28, 191-194, 196-198, 240
  cyclists 79
  pedestrians 7, 18, 22, 24, 28
Penalties *125–128, 134*
Pillion passengers 83, 85, *120*
Police stopping procedures 106
Positioning
  at junctions 175-179, 186, 235
  on the road 160
Powered wheelchairs and powered mobility scooters 36-46, 220, 253
Prohibited vehicles 157-158

Protective clothing 48, 50, 59, 83
Puffin crossings 23-24, 28 191-194, 199, 240
 pedestrians 7, 18, 23-24
 cyclists 79

Q

Quad bikes *see* Prohibited vehicles
Queues 169
 long vehicles 169
 overtaking 163, 288
 pedestrian crossings 192-193
Quiet lanes 206, 218

R

Railway level crossings 34, 167, 243, 291-294
 tactile surfaces 34
Rear-facing baby seats 101
Rear fog lamps 114, 226, 236
Rear view mirrors
 condition 229
 driving 161, 184, 202
 in fog 234-235
Red routes 240, 247, *115*
Reflective clothing
 cyclists 59
 horse riders 50
 motorcyclists 87
 pedestrians 3, 5, 17, 58
 powered mobility vehicles 43
Reflective studs *see* Road studs
Reflectors 48, 60, *118, 128*
Residential area
 lights 115
 pedestrians 152, 206
 speed 152
Restricted drivers *123*
Reversing 200-203, 206, 263

Riding
 cycles 61-82
 horses 52-55
 motorcycles 83-88
Road humps 153
Road junctions 88, 146, 167, 170-183, 211
 cyclists 72-75, 170, 177-180, 182-183
 lanes 177
 parking 243
 pedestrians 8, 170, 180, 206
Road signs *see* Traffic signs/ road markings
Road studs 132
Road traffic law *123-124*
Road users requiring extra care 204-218
Road works 35, 132, 167, 288-290
 contraflow systems 290
 motorways 289
Roundabouts 184-190
 cyclists 76-78, 187
 horse riders 55, 187
 long vehicles 78, 187-188
 mini-roundabouts 186, 188-189
 multiple-roundabouts 190
 road markings 184-185
 specific advice *136-140*
Route guidance and navigation systems 150

S

Safety barriers, pedestrian 9
Safety helmets
 cyclists 59
 horse riders 49
 motorcyclists 83, 86, 283, *132*
School crossing patrols 7, 29, 105, 208, 210

overtaking 167, 209
pole positions *105*
Seat belts 99-100, 102, *128*
Security of vehicles 239, *131*
Separation distance
 cyclists 160, 163, 212
 fog 235
 large vehicles 222
 motorways 260
 overall stopping distance 126, 151, 227, 230, 235, 260, 289
 overtaking 163-164, 222
Shared cycle routes 13, 62
Side winds 232
Signals 103-112
 arm 53, 55, 67, 74, 103, *103-105*
 buses 223
 cyclists 67, 74
 flashing 31, 110-111, 281, 293
 horse riders 53, 55, 215
 junctions 103, 179, 182, 186
 lane changes 133
 large goods vehicles 187
 motorcyclists 88, *103*
 motorways 255-258, 266, 269-270
 moving off 159
 other road users 103-104
 overtaking 163, 267
 pedestrian crossings 22-27, 196, 198-199
 police/wardens/schools/other 105-108, *104-105*
Single carriageways 135-136
Single-track roads 155-156
Skidding 119
 ABS braking 120
 avoiding 231
Slip roads 259, 270, 272-273
Slippery roads *see* Wet/icy slippery roads

Slow-moving traffic 151, 163, 288
Slow-moving vehicles 169, 220, 224-225, 253, 264, 288
 climbing/crawler lanes 139
 flashing amber beacons 225
 level crossings 294
 queues 169
Smoking 148
Snow 228-231
Soft tarmac 237
Speed limiters 222, 265
Speed limits 124-125, 146, 152, 257, 261, 288
Steering condition *128-129*
 winter driving 231
Stopping/parking 238-252
 bus lanes 240
 cycle lanes 140
 level crossings 291, 294
 mobile phones 149
 motorways 91, 240, 270-271
 on footways/footpaths 244, 246
 outside schools 238
 passing places 155-156
 pedestrian crossings 191-192, 196-197, 240
 single-track roads 155-156
Stopping distance 126, 151, 227, 230, 235, 260, 289
 see also Separation distance
Street/footway/footpath repairs 35

T

Tactile paving 10
 surfaces at level crossings 34
Telephones
 mobile phones 149, 278, 283, 285, *131*
 motorways 275, 283

railway 294, 297, 299
Theory test *118-120*
Tinted glasses 94
Tinting, windows *129*
Tiredness/illness 90-91, 237, 262
Toucan crossings 7, 18, 25, 199, 240
  cyclists 61, 80
  pedestrians 7, 25, 80
Towing 98, 160
Traffic calming 153
Traffic lights 109, 184-185, *102*
  cyclists 69, 71, 80-82, 177-178
  green filter lights 177
  junctions 175-178
  level crossings 293, 296
  pedestrians 21
  trams 300-301
Traffic officers
  signals and livery *105*
  stopping procedures 107-108
Traffic signs/road markings 109, 127-131, 134, 142, 143, 184-185, 234, 238, 288, 298, *106-116* **see also** Lines and lanes
  cyclists 63, 69, 71, 140, 178
  junctions 171-172, 174-176, 178, 181, 184
  traffic lights 109, 175-178, *102*
Traffic wardens 7, 105
Trailers 98, 160, 246, 265
Tramways 223, 300-307
  cyclists 82
  overtaking 167, 301
  parking 240, 243, 302
  pedestrians 33, 206, 223, 303
  turning left 183
Transporting animals 98
Triangles 172, 274

Tunnels 126
Turning left
  bus/tram/cycle lanes 183
  junctions 182-183
  one-way streets 143
  roundabouts 186
Turning right
  box junctions 174
  cyclists 74, 212
  diagonal stripes/chevrons 130
  dual carriageways 137, 173
  junctions 179-181
  one-way streets 143
  roundabouts 186
  traffic lights 176-177
Two-second rule 126 **see also** Separation distance
Tyres 227, *118, 129-130*

U

U-turn 188

V

Vehicle condition 89, 97, *128-131*
Vehicle licence *118-122*
Vehicle markings 284-285, *117*
Vehicle registration certificate *122*
Vehicle security 239, *131*
Vehicle tax *122*
Vehicle test certificate (MOT) *121*
Visibility/view 94, 159-160, 162-164, 229, 274
  fog 226, 236
  junctions 88, 170, 211
  lights 114-115, 226, 236
  motorways 235, 267
  overtaking 162-163, 166, 267

pedestrians/cyclists 3, 7, 146, 160, 170
reversing 202, 206
snow 228-229
Vision 92
Vulnerable pedestrians 207

W

Waiting, 238
Warning lights *128*
Water (on brakes) 121
Wet/icy/slippery roads 213, 227-231, 237, 306
pedestrian crossings 195
speed limits 125
stopping distances 126, 227, 230, 260
White lines 127-132, *114*
Windscreens/washers/wipers 229, 235, *128*
Windy weather 232-233
Winter driving *130* **see also** Snow, Wet/icy/slippery roads

Y

Yellow lines 238, 247, *115-116*
Young children 4, 7

Z

Zebra crossings 191-195, 240
cyclists 79
pedestrians 7, 18-20
with a central island 20

Notes

Notes

Notes

Notes

Notes

Notes